P9-DHK-600

a flash
in the pan

a flash in the pan

fast, fabulous recipes in a single skillet

by **brooke dojny** and **melanie barnard**
photographs by **maren caruso**

CHRONICLE BOOKS
SAN FRANCISCO

HIGHLAND PARK PUBLIC LIBRARY
494 LAUREL AVE.
HIGHLAND PARK, IL 60035-2690
847-432-0216

641.77
D658

For Maury, Jennifer, Kristen, and Kristin—the next generation of skillet cooks in our families.

Text copyright © 2003 by Brooke Dojny and Melanie Barnard.
Photographs copyright © 2003 by Maren Caruso.
All rights reserved. No part of this book may be reproduced in any form without written permission from the publisher.

Library of Congress Cataloging-in-Publication Data:

Dojny, Brooke.
  A flash in the pan : fast, fabulous recipes in a single skillet / by Brooke Dojny and Melanie Barnard ; photographs by Maren Caruso.
     p. cm.
  ISBN 0-8118-3578-2
  1. Skillet cookery. 2. Quick and easy cookery. I. Barnard, Melanie. II. Title.
  TX840.S55 D65 2003
  641.7'7—dc21

                            2002005386

Manufactured in China

Food stylists: Erin Quon & Kim Konecny
Photographer's assistant: Saiza Ali
Design and typesetting: Anne Galperin

Distributed in Canada by Raincoast Books
9050 Shaughnessy Street
Vancouver, BC V6P 6E5

10 9 8 7 6 5 4 3 2 1

Chronicle Books LLC
85 Second Street
San Francisco, California 94105

www.chroniclebooks.com

contents

introduction

"In a large skillet . . ." How often over the past dozen years of recipe writing have we begun a recipe with this phrase? In fact, the longer we work on honing our skills at developing fast and easy recipes, the more clearly we understand that the secret to great, quick meals lies in utilizing just this one essential piece of kitchen equipment. Time and again we tell this to beginning cooks who are putting together a kitchen, and also to empty nesters wishing to pare down their kitchen clutter. With a large, good-quality skillet (and a good, sharp knife), dozens of meals can be prepared "from scratch" in no time—and all with a minimum of cleanup.

A Flash in the Pan is a collection of our top 100, personal favorite, skillet main course recipes, all of which can be cooked from start to finish in thirty minutes or less. Organized by main ingredient (Poultry, Pork, Beef, Veal and Lamb, Fish, Shellfish, and Meatless), the recipes utilize all the best of the new, high-quality, shortcut ingredients, without any compromise in taste. Thinly sliced boneless cuts of chicken and meat, fish fillets, shellfish, and the myriad vegetables that now come peeled and prepped form the basis for numerous dishes. High-quality products from the

refrigerator case, such as pre-shredded cheeses and prepared pesto and salsas, are most wel-

come additions. And all the tried and true canned ingredients, such as diced tomatoes (seasoned

or not), chicken and beef broth, and beans are used here without hesitation or apology.

A Flash in the Pan was written for anyone who wants to spend less time than ever shopping

and cleaning up after meals—which is practically everyone. Our well-tested recipes include sautés,

braises, stews, and one-pot wonders such as chicken and rice dishes. They run the gamut from

homey braised pork chops and pan-fried chicken to company-worthy medallions of lamb and

elegant seafood entrees. Fresh herbs and ethnic seasonings—chipotles in adobo, Thai fish

sauce—play important roles in this collection. And each recipe is prefaced by an informational

headnote, complete with suggested accompaniments to round out a meal.

Choosing the Right Skillet

Your grandmother probably has a frying pan, and your mom has a skillet. In the new center of global cuisine, the American kitchen, you might have a sauté pan, and possibly a nonstick one at that. The really good news is that all three of you are using the same basic pan and you can all use the same recipes in whatever pan you have. For centuries, every generation of savvy cooks has known that the best meals can and should be nothing more than a "flash in the pan," from Grandma's legendary corned beef hash to Mom's ultimate comfort scrambled eggs to your up-to-the-minute seared Asian chicken.

Purists will argue that a skillet and a sauté pan are quite different. Yes and no. A frying pan or skillet has low, gently sloping sides, while a sauté pan is a bit deeper, with straighter sides and probably a lid (though you no doubt have a lid in your drawer that fits your skillet, too). We own both a sauté pan, which we use a lot, especially for skillet dishes that have lots of liquid (such as quick stews), and a skillet, which we use even more, especially for any really quick cooking of very thin cuts (such as chicken or veal cutlets). You can, however, use the two pans interchangeably and our recipes work fine cooked in either one. So, for ease and simplicity in using the recipes in this book, we will call all round, flat-bottomed, low-sided, long-handled cooking vessels a skillet. And so can you.

Still, a trip to the kitchenware store can be confusing. In Grandma's day, a cast-iron skillet was probably the only kind available, and Mom branched out into stainless steel or aluminum. Today, however, there are dozens of brands and materials from which to choose. To help you pick the right ones for your needs, here is a quick overview of skillet materials. Note that many skillets (including the ones we recommend) have several layers of different materials.

Copper:
Advantages are excellent heat conductivity and beautiful appearance. Disadvantages are high maintenance, high cost, and limited use as a cooking surface since copper reacts negatively with certain foods. Unlined copper should never be used as a cooking surface.

Aluminum:
Advantages are light weight, excellent heat conductivity, and relatively low cost. Disadvantages are that it is not very strong and metal tools will scratch its surface; limited use as a cooking surface since aluminum reacts negatively with acidic foods. Some aluminum is anodized to strengthen the material and increase scratch resistance, thus improving its usability.

Stainless steel:
Advantages are exceptional durability, scratch resistance, easy-to-clean finish, and moderate cost. Disadvantage is poor heat conductivity.

Cast iron:
Advantages are exceptional durability, low cost, excellent heat retention, especially at high heat. Disadvantages are heavy weight; limited use as a cooking surface since the iron reacts negatively with acid foods; high maintenance, with a periodic seasoning necessary and thorough drying after use to prevent rusting.

Enameled cast iron:
Advantages are low to moderate cost, attractive look, ease of cleaning. Disadvantages are potential chipping and cracking of enamel surface, and tendency of thinner cookware to have "hot spots," while thick cookware is quite heavy.

Because each skillet material has strong advantages and disadvantages, the best cookware on the market uses a combination of materials, usually by layering them into a "sandwich." We especially like skillets that have a stainless steel or anodized aluminum exterior, a stainless steel cooking surface, and bottom core layers or "sandwiches" of aluminum and copper.

Nonstick surfaces are widely available, but the quality varies widely, too. We like nonstick surfaces, especially for medium-size skillets used to make omelets and other egg dishes. We have found that for the most part, however, food does not stick to a good skillet if the pan is properly heated before the food is added. The best nonstick surfaces are those that begin with a high-quality skillet base, and have a durable, slightly rough nonstick coating that promotes good browning and caramelizing of foods.

In addition to the materials, other important features to look for in choosing a skillet are:

★ Good weight and balance so that it is heavy enough to sit flat on an electric or gas burner, but light enough that you will be able to lift it. Larger skillets, and especially sauté pans, often have a small "helper" handle opposite the long handle so that you can lift with two hands.

★ Heat-proof, stainless steel handles that are securely attached to the skillet base.

Cast-iron and enameled cast-iron skillets are usually "cast" of one solid piece and thus have relatively short handles that do get quite hot. It is possible to buy rubber handle "grips" that fit like a permanent, tight glove over these types of handles.

★ If the skillet has a lid, it should fit snugly and firmly and also have a heat-proof, stainless steel handle.

What size skillet should you buy? In our recipes we most often call for a large skillet, which is one that is approximately twelve inches in diameter. It is the ideal and most versatile size for cooking for four people—four pork chops or chicken breasts or hamburgers will fit comfortably in this size skillet. A medium skillet is nine or ten inches in diameter and is perfect for cooking for two; it is also a fine size for making omelets. The size of the pan is measured across the bottom, not the top, which will be wider in a skillet, though top and bottom will be approximately the same in a sauté pan. Actual pan sizes vary a bit from one manufacturer to the next, however. Sauté pans are often sold by volume held, such as a three-quart, but this is inconsistent as well. Though the minimal differences within a pan size rarely matter in a skillet recipe, the better quality ones tend to be more true to size, while less expensive ones are often smaller.

Caring for your skillet is important since this will probably be the most-used and best-loved pan in your kitchen, and the most expensive, too. The key is to read the manufacturer's recommendations and follow them. Good cookware usually comes with a lifetime guarantee, but the manufacturers will honor the guarantee only if the cookware has been properly cared for. Many people put their skillets in the dishwasher. We do not, since most manufacturers don't recommend it, and they just plain take up too much room. Besides, we usually need that favorite pan again before we've run the dishwasher! Storing skillets, stacked, on a shelf saves space and usually causes no harm, but careless stacking can cause surface scratches. If you have space, install a hanging rack so that your skillets can be within easy reach.

Skillet Cooking Basics

The French word *sauter* means "to jump," and that pretty much sums up a lot of skillet cooking. The classic sauté is a cooking process in which thin cuts of meat/poultry/seafood are cooked quickly with a small amount of oil or butter in a hot skillet over medium or high heat. Just the ticket for those of us with big flavor ideas and tight cooking schedules. Here is a quick primer on how to get the most out of your skillet cooking:

Be sure the food to be cooked is of even thickness for even cooking. Tender cuts can often be flattened with the palm of your hand or between pieces of plastic wrap.

Pat the food dry if it is to be panfried or browned in the skillet. Moist food will steam rather than caramelize and brown.

Heat the skillet with the butter or oil before adding the food. Most sticking occurs because the meat is put in a cold skillet and then heated. For the classic "jump," heat that pan first.

Leave space, at least ½ inch, between pieces of meat/poultry/seafood that are to be browned. If they are too close together, they will steam instead.

Avoid the temptation to flip the food in the pan. Turn only when the first side is properly browned, which will also go a long way toward the prevention of food sticking. In most cases, the food needs to be turned only once during cooking.

Never wash out a skillet with caramelized, crusty browned bits on the bottom. These are the bases for practically every good pan sauce. Instead, deglaze the skillet by adding some liquid, raising the heat to high, and scraping up the browned bits as they "melt" into the bubbly liquid. You may serve this quick and easy sauce unadorned, or with herbs added, or boiled for a few minutes to reduce and concentrate it. Most of our sauté recipes incorporate this classic deglazing technique.

Shop for a skillet as you would for a fine article of clothing. Try it on your hand to see if it is comfortable and well balanced for lifting. Store and care for the skillet as you would your best outfit—not too close to other items and washed according to the manufacturer's label. Treasure your skillet as you would your best piece of jewelry—use it every day and not just for special occasions. Like your favorite classic suit, your skillet will always be in good taste and last a lifetime.

The
Flash
Pantry

With a well-stocked pantry, refrigerator, and freezer, dinner is always right at hand.

Use this list to stock your kitchen according to your own preferences, supplementing with herbs, greens, fish and other seafood, and other fresh ingredients weekly.

In the Refrigerator

Butter
Carrots
Celery
Cheddar cheese and other softer shredding
  cheeses
Eggs
Ginger
Lemons
Limes
Milk
Nuts (or store in freezer)
Parmesan cheese and other hard grating
  cheeses
Pesto sauce
Plain yogurt
Salsa
Sour cream, and whipping or heavy cream
  for special dishes
Sturdy lettuce such as romaine

In the Root Vegetable Bin

Garlic
Onions
Potatoes—new and russet
Shallots

continued

The Flash Pantry *continued*

In the Freezer

Breads
Chicken breasts and thighs
Corn
Ground beef and other frequently used meats
Ice cream/sorbet
Peas
Sausages
Spinach
Tortillas

On the Pantry Shelf

Anchovies
Broth—Beef and Chicken
Canned beans—black, kidney, white, chickpeas
Canned coconut milk
Capers
Couscous
Diced and whole canned tomatoes
Dried bread crumbs
Dried fruit
Dried herbs and ground spices
Fish sauce
Green chiles
Hoisin sauce
Ketchup
Liquid hot-pepper sauce, such as Tabasco
Mayonnaise
Mustards—regular and coarse-grain
Olive oil—extra-virgin and light
Olives
Pasta—strands and other shapes
Rice—long-grain and Arborio
Soy sauce
Toasted sesame oil
Tomato sauce
Tuna, preferably oil-packed
Vegetable oil
Vinegars—red wine, white wine, and balsamic
Wine—red, white, and sherry
Worcestershire sauce

poultry

The meat department at the supermarket really ought to be renamed the "chicken department" since this bird, in dozens of assorted parts and versions, dominates the meat case everywhere. In fact, chicken is America's favorite bird and favorite supper, too. With its endless versatility, modest cost, and universal appeal, chicken is our pick for easy family meals. Coming in not far behind is turkey, which we all know is not just for Thanksgiving anymore.

Indeed, it is the "invention" of boneless, skinless chicken breasts (there are kids, these days, who think chickens have no bones) that has revolutionized home cooking. In the old days (about fifteen years ago), you had to painstakingly bone and skin chicken yourself, and it was a messy job. Today, however, we can buy not only breasts, but boneless, skinless thighs and skinless legs, too. Though these "naked" chicken pieces lose a bit of natural flavor provided by the skin and bones, their very neutrality and lower fat content are what make them so versatile and able to adapt to so many recipes.

Poultry is important in every major world cuisine, and Americans are increasingly interested in easy adaptations of exotic dishes. So, in addition to quick and easy versions of all-American favorites like Buttermilk Fried Chicken and Gravy (page 31), and Skillet Chicken and Chive Dumplings (page 36), we offer Quick Coq au Vin (page 26), and Thai-Style Ginger Chicken Stir-Fry (page 32)

recipes

chicken with sweet peppers and balsamic vinegar *4 servings*

If the number of times a dish is made is the measure of how much we like it, then this is our favorite. Everyone in both of our families loves it; this was the first recipe each of the children wanted when leaving home, skillet in hand. With a side of plain pasta, a hunk of good bread, and a simple green salad, it is the perfect midweek supper. Make a pasta with thin strands, such as cappellini, and swirl it into nests; add a cruet of good olive oil for the bread; sprinkle some Gorgonzola on the salad; and it becomes a dinner fit for a Saturday night with friends. What makes this simple dish so wonderful is the rainbow of sweet pepper colors, an abundance of fresh herbs, and a splash of "top shelf" balsamic vinegar—the pricey stuff that costs at least ten dollars per bottle and is worth every penny. A real timesaving tip—buy the array of colorful peppers already sliced at the supermarket salad bar.

4 skinless, boneless chicken breast halves
   Salt and freshly ground pepper
4 tablespoons olive oil
4 cups thinly sliced mixed red, yellow, orange, and/or green bell peppers
1 medium onion, thinly sliced
4 large garlic cloves, finely chopped
¼ cup chopped fresh basil
3 tablespoons high-quality balsamic vinegar

Season the chicken with salt and pepper. In a large skillet, heat 2 tablespoons of the oil. Sauté the chicken over medium-high heat, turning once, until golden on both sides, about 8 minutes total. Transfer the chicken to a plate.

Add the remaining 2 tablespoons of oil to the skillet and reduce the heat to medium. Cook the bell peppers and onion, stirring often, until just softened, about 4 minutes. Add the garlic and cook, stirring, for 1 minute. Stir in about half of the basil and the vinegar. Return the chicken and any accumulated juices to the skillet. Reduce the heat to medium-low. Simmer until the chicken is cooked through, about 3 minutes. Stir in the remaining basil and season with salt and pepper.

double
mustard chicken
paillards *4 servings*

Mustard seeds become mellower with cooking. The crunch of the seeds and the smoothness of the honey mustard cream sauce make this a rather sophisticated little dish. But since almost everyone, kids included, loves mustard, it will also have a lot of family appeal. Mustard and broccoli go well together, so that's what we'd serve with the chicken, along with a nice rice pilaf—some of the mixes on the market now are really good.

1¼ pounds thinly sliced chicken breast cutlets
    Salt and freshly ground pepper
 1 tablespoon whole mustard seeds
 3 tablespoons butter
⅓ cup dry white wine
⅓ cup chicken broth
¼ cup heavy cream
1½ tablespoons honey mustard

Season the chicken with salt and pepper, then sprinkle evenly with the mustard seeds, patting them into the chicken.

In a large skillet, heat the butter. Sauté the chicken over medium-high heat, turning once, until golden and cooked through, about 5 minutes total. Transfer the chicken to a plate

Add the wine and broth to the skillet and bring to a simmer, stirring up browned bits clinging to the bottom of the pan. Reduce the heat to medium-low, simmer for 1 minute, then stir in the cream and honey mustard. Simmer again for 1 minute. Return the chicken and accumulated juices to the skillet. Simmer until the chicken is heated through, about 1 minute more. Season to taste with salt and pepper

chicken country captain *4 servings*

The story in Georgia goes like this: A British army officer (the "captain") brought the recipe back to his Georgia home (the "country") after his posting in India. As usual, South Carolina disputes Georgia. In the low country, they swear that the dish originated in Savannah, a major shipping port for spices. The only points of agreement are that the dish's origins are Indian, pretty obvious with the curry base, and that it was adapted to American tastes with its arrival here. Being from New England, we don't have any desire to enter into any conflict again with the South, so we will just tell you that Chicken Country Captain is an all-American classic, here presented in a quick, but no less tasty version. Plain white rice mixed with a spoonful of bottled chutney complements the curry, and cornbread is always good with bacon.

- ¼ cup slivered almonds
- 4 bacon slices, cut into 1-inch pieces
- 4 skinless, boneless chicken thighs
  Salt and freshly ground pepper
- 1 medium onion, thinly sliced
- 1 medium green bell pepper, thinly sliced
- 3 large garlic cloves, finely chopped
- 2 teaspoons curry powder
- One 14½-ounce can diced tomatoes
- ½ cup chicken broth
- ¼ cup dried currants
- 2 tablespoons chopped fresh thyme

In a large, deep skillet with a lid, toss the almonds over medium heat until golden and fragrant. Transfer to a plate and set aside. In the same skillet, cook the bacon over medium heat, stirring often, until crisp. Drain on paper towels, and set aside, leaving the bacon drippings in the pan. Season the chicken lightly with salt and generously with pepper. Raise the heat to medium-high and cook the chicken in the bacon drippings, turning once, until golden on both sides, about 8 minutes total. Transfer the chicken to a plate.

Add the onion and bell pepper to skillet. Reduce the heat to medium and cook, stirring often, until the vegetables are softened, about 5 minutes. Add the garlic and curry powder, and cook 1 minute. Stir in the tomatoes, broth, currants, and 1 tablespoon of the thyme. Return the chicken and any accumulated juices to the pan. Cover and simmer until the chicken is cooked through, 10 to 15 minutes. Stir in the remaining thyme. Season to taste with salt and pepper. (The chicken may be prepared up to 4 hours ahead of time and refrigerated. Reheat gently to serve.)

Serve the chicken and sauce sprinkled with the reserved almonds and bacon.

summertime chicken sauté with tomato-caper coulis *4 servings*

Medium-high heat is essential here in order to ensure that the thin, tender chicken cutlets are quickly seared to a golden hue, which adds flavor and seals in natural juices at the same time. This Provençal-style dish is lovely accompanied by grilled zucchini and eggplant, an orzo salad from the deli, and sliced apricots steeped in sweet wine for dessert.

1¼ pounds thinly sliced chicken breast cutlets
    Salt and freshly ground pepper
¼ cup extra-virgin olive oil
½ cup coarsely chopped shallots
¾ pound tomatoes, seeded and chopped
    (about 3 cups)
½ cup dry white wine
1½ tablespoons small capers plus 1 tablespoon liquid
1½ tablespoons chopped fresh rosemary,
    plus sprigs for garnish

Season the chicken with salt and pepper. In a large skillet, heat the oil. Sauté the chicken over medium-high heat, turning once, until golden and cooked through, about 5 minutes total. Transfer the chicken to a plate.

Add the shallots to the drippings in the pan, reduce the heat to medium, and cook, stirring, for 1 minute. Add the tomatoes, wine, capers and liquid, and chopped rosemary. Simmer, stirring occasionally, until the tomatoes begin to give up their juices, 3 to 4 minutes. Return the chicken and accumulated juices to skillet and heat just until warmed, about 1 minute. Season to taste with salt and pepper.

Serve the chicken with the tomato coulis spooned over the top.

chicken with wild mushroom ragout *4 servings*

These days, all sorts of fresh wild mushrooms are as prolific in our markets as are the boring white button variety. What's really great, however, is that wild mushrooms are no longer double-digit in price. Maybe they are not so wild anymore. No matter, because they taste great and are generally interchangeable in recipes. So feel free to use shiitake, oyster, chanterelle, or porcini, or a combination of these and flavorful culti-vated mushrooms such as portobello or cremini. There is plenty of mushroom sauce here, enough to spill over onto a side dish of orzo. Round out the plate with steamed asparagus, which shares a natural season and affinity with many mushrooms.

4 skinless, boneless chicken breast halves
   Salt and freshly ground pepper
3 tablespoons butter
¼ cup finely chopped shallots
1 pound fresh wild mushrooms or a mix of wild
      and cultivated mushrooms, trimmed and sliced
3 tablespoons Madeira or dry sherry
1 tablespoon Worcestershire sauce
2 tablespoons chopped fresh tarragon

Season the chicken with salt and pepper. In a large skillet with a lid, heat 2 tablespoons of the butter. Cook the chicken over medium-high heat, turning once, until golden on both sides, about 8 minutes total. Transfer the chicken to a plate.

Add the remaining 1 tablespoon of butter to the skillet and reduce the heat to medium. Cook the shallots and mushrooms, stirring often, until the mushrooms are softened and beginning to release their juices, about 4 minutes. Add the Madeira, Worcester-shire sauce, and half of the tarragon. Cook, stirring, until the mushrooms are completely soft, about 2 minutes more. Stir in the remaining tarragon, then return the chicken and accumulated juices to the pan. Reduce the heat to medium-low, cover, and simmer until the chicken is cooked through, 4 to 5 minutes. Season to taste with salt and pepper.

lemon asparagus chicken stir-fry *4 servings*

Woks are great, but a good heavy skillet does a beautiful stir-fry, too. The key is the quality of the skillet —good ones conduct high heat evenly and thoroughly. The other important component to a stir-fry is having all the ingredients ready beforehand since the cooking itself takes only a few minutes, but must be done from start to finish without stopping. That all seems like a recipe for really quick cooking, but some stir-fries have you chopping and dicing for an hour ahead of time! Not so here. You can buy the chicken breast already sliced for stir-frying, and the bell pepper sliced and ready from the salad bar, thus saving loads of time. Serve this colorful main dish with a golden rice pilaf and a salad of mixed spring greens.

- 1 large lemon
- 1¼ pounds boneless, skinless chicken breasts, cut into thin strips
- Salt and freshly ground pepper
- 4 tablespoons peanut or vegetable oil
- 1 pound thin asparagus, trimmed and cut into 1½-inch diagonal slices
- 1 small red bell pepper, thinly sliced
- 4 garlic cloves, finely chopped
- ⅔ cup chicken broth
- 2 tablespoons soy sauce
- ¼ teaspoon crushed red pepper flakes

Grate 2 teaspoons of zest from the lemon, squeeze 2 tablespoons of juice, and set aside. Season the chicken lightly with salt and pepper. In a large skillet, heat 2 tablespoons of the oil over high heat. Stir-fry the chicken, stirring constantly, until golden and nearly cooked through, about 4 minutes. Use a slotted spoon to transfer the chicken to a plate.

Add the remaining 2 tablespoons of oil to the skillet and cook the asparagus and bell pepper, stirring constantly, until crisp-tender, about 1 minute. Add the garlic and cook 30 seconds. Add the broth, soy sauce, pepper flakes, and the reserved lemon juice and zest. Return the chicken and accumulated juices to the pan. Reduce the heat to medium-low and simmer until the chicken is cooked through, about 2 minutes. Season to taste with salt and pepper.

quick
coq au vin *4 servings*

Though it is commonly thought that French food is all
complexity and cream, coq au vin is the essence of true
French cooking—fine ingredients treated well. The
name of the dish translates simply as "chicken in
wine," and the recipe is dependent on the quality of
both. Though this recipe is streamlined and designed
to cook more quickly, it is still the caliber of chicken,
bacon, wine, and herbs that produces the impressive
results. Stay with the classics by accompanying this
company-worthy main course with roasted potatoes
and steamed slim green beans, and end with an apple
tart from your favorite bakery.

4 bacon slices, cut into 1-inch pieces
4 bone-in chicken breast halves
 Salt and freshly ground pepper
2 cups frozen pearl onions, thawed
1⅓ cups hearty red wine
⅔ cup chicken broth
2 tablespoons chopped fresh thyme,
 plus whole sprigs for garnish

In a large, deep skillet with a lid, cook the bacon over
medium heat, stirring often, until browned and crisp,
4 to 6 minutes. Drain on paper towels, leaving the
drippings in the skillet.

Season the chicken lightly with salt and generously with pepper. Sauté the chicken in the bacon
drippings over medium-high heat, turning once, until
golden brown on both sides, about 8 minutes total.
Transfer the chicken to a plate.

Add the onions to the pan and cook, stirring
often, until golden, about 4 minutes. Add the wine,
broth, and 1 tablespoon of the chopped thyme, stirring and scraping up the browned bits on the bottom
of the pan until the mixture is simmering. Return the
chicken and any accumulated juices to the pan. Cover,
reduce the heat to medium-low, and simmer until the
chicken is cooked through, about 15 minutes.

Transfer the chicken to a plate. Stir the remaining
1 tablespoon of chopped thyme into the pan sauce.
Raise the heat to medium-high and cook, stirring often,
until the sauce is slightly reduced, about 2 minutes.
Stir in the reserved bacon and season to taste with salt
and pepper.

Serve the chicken with the sauce spooned over,
and garnish with thyme sprigs.

red curry chicken sauté with coconut and lime *4 servings*

There is lots of savory broth in this Thai-inspired dish, so pair it with rice noodles and some French bread to mop it up. (Thailand and France have a long culinary history together.) Red curry paste and canned coconut milk are just a few of the many Thai ingredients stocked in the supermarket. Get to know this section of the store, as these ingredients can be the basis of all sorts of interesting sautés or stir-fries. We also like the dish with green curry paste, which is just about as peppery as red, but quite different in flavor.

  1 large lime
  4 skinless, boneless chicken breast halves
    Salt and freshly ground pepper
  3 tablespoons peanut or vegetable oil
1½ tablespoons red curry paste
  1 cup canned unsweetened coconut milk
⅔ cup chicken broth
  2 cups snow peas, strings removed
  1 cup sliced green onions

Grate 2 teaspoons of zest from the lime and squeeze 2 tablespoons of juice. Reserve the zest and juice. Season the chicken with salt and pepper.

In a large skillet, heat the oil. Sauté the chicken over medium-high heat, turning once, until golden, about 8 minutes total. Transfer the chicken to a plate.

Stir the curry paste into the pan drippings, then stir in the coconut milk and chicken broth. Bring to a simmer, stirring up the browned bits clinging to the bottom of the pan. Stir in the lime juice and zest, then return the chicken and accumulated juices to the pan. Reduce the heat to medium-low and simmer until the chicken is just cooked through, about 5 minutes more. Stir in the snow peas and half of the green onions. Simmer until the snow peas are crisp-tender, about 2 minutes. Stir in the remaining green onions. Season to taste with salt and pepper.

tuscan chicken rolls *4 servings*

If you want a really elegant chicken dish that's fast, easy, and will impress even the most finicky of guests, this is for you. The only real work is flattening out the chicken, and that's a breeze if you put the breasts between pieces of plastic wrap and use that versatile skillet to press them flat. We love this summery Italian combination of mozzarella, prosciutto, roasted peppers, and fresh basil; but other appealing options might be ham, Swiss cheese, and tarragon; or smoked salmon, Gouda, and dill. We suggest that you serve this Tuscan version with a little spaghettini tossed with olive oil, garlic, and fresh plum tomatoes; an arugula salad; and a finale of raspberry gelato.

4 skinless, boneless chicken breast halves
  Salt and freshly ground pepper
2 thin slices prosciutto, cut in half crosswise
8 large basil leaves
1 roasted red pepper (from a jar, from the deli, or fresh), cut into 4 pieces
2 ounces mozzarella cheese
3 tablespoons extra-virgin olive oil
⅓ cup Marsala wine
⅓ cup chicken broth

Place the chicken breast halves, one at a time, between pieces of heavy plastic wrap. With a heavy skillet, meat mallet, or rolling pin, pound the chicken to an even thickness of less than ½ inch. Season the chicken with salt and pepper. Place a quarter of the prosciutto, basil, red pepper, and cheese in the center of each piece of chicken, then roll into a cylinder, tucking in the ends. Secure each chicken roll with a toothpick, though the chicken will tend to stay closed on its own.

In a large skillet with a lid, heat the oil. Cook the chicken over medium heat, turning carefully with tongs so all sides are golden and the chicken is nearly cooked through, about 12 minutes total. Transfer the chicken to a plate.

Add the Marsala and broth to the skillet, stirring up browned bits clinging to the bottom. Bring to a boil, then return the chicken and accumulated juices to the skillet. Cover and simmer until the chicken is cooked through, about 5 minutes longer. Uncover, raise the heat to high, and reduce the sauce slightly, about 1 minute. Season the sauce with salt and pepper.

bacon and cheddar chicken *4 servings*

When they were young, this was the kids' favorite weeknight chicken dish. Now they are grown and gone, and it is still their favorite. Take note, you empty-nest parents—this recipe works. Brings them home every time, especially when served on top of shredded lettuce tossed with creamy Italian dressing (think BLT), with a little spaghetti and tomato sauce on the side. A slice of chocolate layer cake for dessert would be an added incentive.

4 bacon slices
4 skinless, boneless chicken breast halves
   Salt and freshly ground pepper
1 large egg, beaten
1 cup unseasoned bread crumbs, preferably panko crumbs (see Note)
1 tablespoon chopped fresh marjoram
4 tomato slices
¾ cup shredded cheddar cheese

In a large skillet with a lid, cook the bacon over medium heat until crisp and browned, about 10 minutes. Drain on paper towels. Reserve the pan drippings and set the bacon aside.

Season the chicken with salt and pepper, then dip into the egg to coat. On a plate, combine the bread crumbs with the marjoram. Dredge the chicken in the crumbs to coat completely.

Cook the chicken over medium heat in the pan drippings, turning once, until the crumbs are browned and the chicken is cooked through, 12 to 15 minutes. Place a tomato slice atop each chicken breast half, then break the bacon slices in half and crisscross over the tomato. Sprinkle evenly with the cheese. Cover the pan, reduce the heat to medium-low, and cook until the tomato slices are heated through and the cheese is melted, 1 to 2 minutes.

note:
Panko are light, very crisp Japanese bread crumbs.

buttermilk fried chicken and gravy *4 servings*

Much maligned but still much loved, fried chicken doesn't have to be shunned by health-conscious cooks. Just lose the skin and keep the crunch. Boneless chicken breasts, dipped in buttermilk, coated in corn-meal, and skillet fried in a touch of oil take about 15 minutes from start to finish. This is our hands-down favorite way to make fried chicken. The secret is the buttermilk—but then every cook who makes fried chicken already knows that. Mashed potatoes swirled with chopped green onions and plain steamed spinach are the ideal accompaniments. A traditional chicken-frying cook always seems to be a lemon meringue pie baker, too. No argument with that—we gave the chicken recipe to our bakery and they gave us a pie. Cooperation at its finest.

- 1 cup buttermilk
- 1 pound boneless, skinless chicken breasts, cut into 2-inch chunks
- ¼ cup yellow cornmeal
- ¼ cup plus 2 tablespoons all-purpose flour
- 1 teaspoon coarsely ground pepper
- ½ teaspoon salt
- ¼ cup corn or canola oil
- 1 cup chicken broth
- 1 teaspoon hot-pepper sauce, or to taste

Pour ½ cup of the buttermilk into a shallow dish just large enough to hold the chicken. Use your hand to flatten the chicken to an even thickness of about ½ inch. Dip the chicken in the buttermilk, turning to coat completely. In another shallow dish, combine the cornmeal, ¼ cup of the flour, the pepper, and salt. Dredge the chicken in the cornmeal, patting the mix-ture to coat the chicken all over.

In a large skillet, heat the oil. Panfry the chicken over medium-high heat, turning once, until it is cooked through and the coating is dark golden brown, about 8 minutes total. Transfer the chicken to a plate.

Stir the remaining 2 tablespoons of flour into the pan drippings and cook, stirring constantly, until the flour paste takes on a golden color, about 2 minutes. Whisk in the broth and remaining ½ cup of butter-milk. Cook, stirring up the browned bits on the bottom of the pan, until the gravy is bubbly. Reduce the heat to medium-low and continue to cook, stir-ring, for 2 minutes. Season with hot-pepper sauce, salt, and pepper.

Serve the chicken with the gravy ladled over it.

thai-style ginger chicken stir-fry *4 servings*

Fish sauce is the salt and pepper of Thai cooking. Whiffed from the bottle, it smells awful, but incorporated into stir-fries and other recipes, it is the secret essential ingredient that makes people love Thai food. Combine fish sauce with ginger, cilantro, and lemongrass for a stir-fry that is the essence of Thai flavors, prepared quickly, American-style. If you can't find lemongrass, first hound your produce person to get this wonderfully lemon-perfumed fresh woody herb. If that fails, use 2 teaspoons of grated lemon zest and 1 tablespoon of fresh lemon juice in its place. Or use reconstituted dried lemongrass. Accompany with a mound of steamed jasmine or white rice studded with peanuts, or turn this stir-fry into a salad by serving it on a bed of shredded romaine lettuce.

1¼ pounds skinless, boneless chicken breasts, cut into thin strips
Salt and freshly ground pepper
3 tablespoons peanut or vegetable oil
3 large garlic cloves, finely chopped
2 tablespoons finely chopped fresh ginger
2 tablespoons chopped fresh lemongrass (white part only)
1 cup thinly sliced green onions
⅔ cup chicken broth
1½ tablespoons Thai fish sauce
3 tablespoons chopped cilantro

Season the chicken lightly with salt and pepper. In a large skillet, heat the oil over high heat. Stir-fry the chicken, stirring constantly, until golden and nearly cooked through, about 4 minutes. Stir in the garlic, ginger, and lemongrass and cook, stirring, for 30 seconds. Add about half of the green onions, the broth, and fish sauce. Reduce the heat to medium and simmer until the chicken is cooked through and the sauce is slightly reduced, 2 to 3 minutes. Stir in the remaining green onions and the cilantro.

chicken tomatillo chile verde *4 servings*

Tomatillos are often confused with American green tomatoes. Though they are from the same plant family, tomatillos are green when fully ripe and have a distinct, very tart, lemony taste that is not very palatable raw, but mellows and deepens upon cooking. Here tomatillos are teamed with green chiles, cilantro, and green onions, and the result is truly a *verde* ("green") sauce. For contrast, serve it with red beans and rice, and don't forget lots of warmed corn tortillas.

1¼ pounds skinless, boneless chicken breasts,
     cut into 1½-inch chunks
     Salt
  3 tablespoons yellow cornmeal
  1 tablespoon chili powder
  ¼ cup corn or vegetable oil
  2 cups chicken broth
  1 cup drained canned tomatillos
One 2-ounce can chopped green chiles, with the liquid
  ½ cup thinly sliced green onions
  ⅓ cup chopped fresh cilantro
     Freshly ground pepper

Season the chicken with salt. On a plate, combine the cornmeal and chili powder. Roll the chicken in the cornmeal mixture to coat. Reserve any cornmeal remaining on plate.

In a large skillet, heat the oil. Cook the chicken over medium-high heat, turning once, until golden and nearly cooked through, about 6 minutes. Transfer the chicken to a plate.

Stir 1 tablespoon of the reserved cornmeal into the pan, then add the broth, tomatillos, and green chiles. Bring to a simmer, then reduce the heat to medium and simmer until slightly reduced and thickened, 3 to 4 minutes. Return the chicken to the pan, and add the green onions and cilantro. Simmer until the chicken is heated through, about 2 minutes. Season to taste with salt and pepper. (The chicken can be prepared up to 2 hours ahead and held at cool room temperature or refrigerated. Reheat gently to serve.)

moroccan braised chicken and dried fruits *4 servings*

Figs, apricots, and plums are abundant throughout the Middle East and are frequently used in spicy, savory dishes. Mixed dried fruits are available in bags in the United States, and whatever combination you can find will be delightful here. Salty green olives and the combination of cumin and coriander lend the dish its irresistible aroma and appeal. Fluffy couscous studded with almonds, and grilled or steamed zucchini slices round out the plate. Pistachio ice cream is the perfect dessert.

4 bone-in chicken thighs or legs
  Salt
1 teaspoon ground cumin
1 teaspoon ground coriander
3 tablespoons olive oil
4 garlic cloves, finely chopped
1 cup dry white wine
1 cup chicken broth
1¼ cups mixed dried fruits (about 6 ounces)
½ cup pitted and halved brine-cured green olives
  Freshly ground pepper

Season the chicken with salt, the cumin, and coriander. In a large skillet with a lid, heat the oil. Cook the chicken over medium-high heat, turning once, until golden brown, about 8 minutes total. Transfer the chicken to a plate.

Add the garlic to the pan and cook, stirring about 30 seconds. Add the wine and broth, stirring up the browned bits clinging to the bottom of the pan. Add the fruits and bring to a simmer. Return the chicken and accumulated juices to the skillet. Reduce the heat to medium-low, cover, and simmer gently until the chicken is cooked through and the fruits are tender, 15 to 18 minutes. Uncover, add the olives, and simmer until the sauce is slightly reduced, 2 to 3 minutes. Season to taste with salt and pepper. (The chicken may be prepared up to 4 hours ahead and held at cool room temperature or refrigerated. Reheat gently to serve.)

basque garlic chicken and rice *4 servings*

The fiercely independent Basques of Spain have a cuisine all their own, based on the farming practices and products of their mountainous terrain. Basque shepherds immigrated to the western mountains of the United States and brought the lusty cooking of their people with them. Garlic (lots of it), roasted peppers, and full-flavored meats and poultry are mainstays of many dishes, and this adaptation of a simple classic doesn't stray from these Basque flavors. A one-dish supper, all it needs is a hearty salad of romaine lettuce with a red wine vinaigrette and a basket of crusty bread. Spaniards like to end a spicy meal with a soothing custard, so vanilla pudding would work well.

8 chicken drumsticks or 4 bone-in chicken thighs
Salt and freshly ground pepper
¼ cup olive oil
4 ounces chorizo sausage, thickly sliced,
    or 4 ounces smoked ham, cubed
1 large onion, coarsely chopped
6 large garlic cloves, finely chopped
1 cup white rice
2 cups chicken broth, plus ¼ to ½ cup as needed
1 cup coarsely chopped roasted red pepper
1 cup frozen green peas

Season the chicken with salt and pepper. In a large, deep skillet with a lid, heat the oil. Cook the chicken and chorizo over medium-high heat, turning once, until golden, about 8 minutes total. Transfer to a plate.

Add the onion to the skillet, reduce the heat to medium, and cook, stirring often, until nearly softened. Add the garlic and cook, stirring, 1 minute. Stir in the rice and cook, stirring, until coated with oil, about 1 minute. Stir in the broth, then return the chicken and sausage and any accumulated juices to the skillet. Bring to a simmer, then reduce the heat to medium-low, cover the pan, and simmer 15 minutes. Gently stir in the roasted pepper and peas. If all the liquid is absorbed, add ¼ to ½ cup additional broth. Cover and simmer until the rice is tender, the liquid is absorbed, and the chicken is cooked through, 5 to 7 minutes more. Season to taste with salt and pepper. (The chicken may be prepared up to 2 hours ahead and held at cool room temperature or refrigerated. Reheat in a microwave oven, adding additional broth if the rice seems dry.)

skillet chicken and chive dumplings *4 servings*

Chicken and dumplings is a staple in Pennsylvania Dutch country, where Melanie's maternal grandmother was born and raised. Grandma, an extraordinary cook and a forward-thinking woman, was an early fan of Bisquick, one of the first real convenience foods on the market. This modern woman of the Depression era figured it had all the same things she used to make dumplings—flour, shortening, buttermilk, and leavening—which she had a hard time getting during those years. As a working mom, she also prized the idea of saving time. So, in honor of Grandma, we continue the Bisquick tradition, but add the even greater time savers of store-sliced carrots and celery, and butcher-prepared boneless chicken. Grandma served her chicken and dumplings with steamed green peas and baked apples (and the apples weren't even dessert—grandmas are really smart). No need to change that.

1 pound skinless, boneless chicken thighs, cut into 1½-inch chunks
    Salt and freshly ground pepper
3 tablespoons butter
2 cups thinly sliced carrots
2 cups thinly sliced celery
3 cups chicken broth
2 tablespoons chopped fresh mixed herbs, such as marjoram, mint, and/or thyme
1½ cups buttermilk baking mix, such as Bisquick
½ cup milk
¼ cup plus 2 tablespoons snipped chives

Season the chicken lightly with salt and pepper. In a large, deep skillet with a lid, heat the butter. Cook the chicken over medium-high heat, turning once, until golden on both sides, about 8 minutes total. Transfer the chicken to a plate.

Add the carrots and celery to the skillet. Reduce the heat to medium and cook, stirring often, until the vegetables are softened, about 5 minutes. Return the chicken to the pan, add the broth and 1 tablespoon of the chopped herbs, and bring to a simmer. (The chicken may be prepared to this point up to 4 hours ahead and held at cool room temperature or refrigerated. Reheat before adding the dumplings.)

In a mixing bowl, stir together the baking mix, milk, remaining 1 tablespoon of mixed herbs, and 2 tablespoons of the chives and continue stirring until a soft dough forms. Drop the dough by heaping teaspoons onto the simmering stew. Cover, reduce the heat to medium-low, and simmer until the dumplings are puffy and cooked through, 15 to 17 minutes. Gently stir in the remaining ¼ cup of chives. Season to taste with salt and pepper.

turkey with herbed country pan gravy *4 servings*

This is Thanksgiving dinner for any Thursday of the year. The seasoning and gravy are the same, and the whole thing takes about 10 minutes from start to finish. The rest of the meal is pretty obvious—mashed potatoes (there is plenty of gravy), cornbread stuffing (from a mix is fine, just add some fresh herbs), cranberry sauce, and pumpkin pie from the bakery.

1¼ pounds turkey breast cutlets
    Salt and freshly ground pepper
2 teaspoons poultry seasoning
4 tablespoons butter
1 large celery rib, coarsely chopped
1 medium onion, coarsely chopped
2 tablespoons all-purpose flour
1¾ cups chicken broth
2 tablespoons chopped fresh sage,
    plus whole leaves for garnish

Season the turkey with salt, pepper, and 1 teaspoon of the poultry seasoning. In a large skillet, heat 2 tablespoons of the butter. Sauté the turkey over medium-high heat, turning once, until golden on both sides, 6 to 8 minutes total. Transfer the turkey to a plate.

Add the remaining 2 tablespoons of butter to skillet and reduce the heat to medium. Cook the celery and onion, stirring often, until softened. Stir in the flour and remaining teaspoon of poultry seasoning. Cook, stirring constantly, for 1 minute. Add the broth and 1 tablespoon of the chopped sage. Cook, stirring constantly, until the gravy is thickened and bubbly. Return the turkey and accumulated juices to the skillet. Add the remaining tablespoon of chopped sage. Simmer until the turkey is heated through, about 1 minute. Season to taste with salt and pepper.

Serve the turkey and gravy garnished with sage leaves.

turkey with chipotle mole
4 servings

Chipotles, which are dried smoked jalapeños, are available whole, ground, or canned in a spicy adobo sauce. For the most flavor punch with the least work, we like the canned chipotles in adobo. Mole, perhaps the national dish of Mexico, is said to have been invented by nuns whose bishop unexpectedly came to the convent for dinner. With only a turkey on hand, the nuns concocted a complicated sauce from ingredients they had—chiles and other spices, seeds, almonds, tomatoes, tortillas, and unsweetened chocolate. The unlikely combination was an instant hit, and the recipe (or variations on it) spread throughout the land. Here is a very streamlined, very quick version, using few ingredients, but with a complex flavor owed to the spicy, rich adobo sauce canned with the chipotles. Serve this with rice, corn tortillas, and a spinach salad with orange segments tossed in.

2 teaspoons whole cumin seeds
1¼ pounds turkey breast or thigh cutlets
    Salt and freshly ground pepper
4 tablespoons olive oil
1 large onion, thinly sliced
One 14¼-ounce can stewed tomatoes with green
        chiles, or Mexican-style stewed tomatoes
½ cup chicken broth
2 canned chipotles in adobo, chopped, plus
        1 tablespoon or more adobo sauce
½ ounce unsweetened chocolate, chopped

Place the cumin seeds in a sturdy plastic bag, then use a mallet or rolling pin to partially crush them. Season the turkey with salt and pepper, then sprinkle with the seeds, using your hand to pat them into the turkey meat. In a large skillet, heat 2 tablespoons of the oil. Cook the turkey over medium-high heat, turning once, until golden on both sides, about 8 minutes total. Transfer the turkey to a plate.

Add the remaining 2 tablespoons of olive oil and the onion to the skillet. Reduce the heat to medium and cook the onion, stirring often, until softened and tinged with gold, 6 to 7 minutes. Add the tomatoes and their juices, the broth, chipotles and adobo sauce, and chocolate. Bring to a simmer, then reduce the heat to medium-low and simmer 2 minutes. Return the turkey and any accumulated juices to the skillet and simmer until the sauce is slightly reduced and the turkey is cooked through, 3 to 4 minutes. Season to taste with salt and pepper. (The dish can be cooked up to 3 hours ahead and held at cool room temperature or refrigerated. Reheat gently.)

turkey cutlets with cranberry wine sauce *4 servings*

Turkey and cranberries have had a long-standing love affair, which we don't think should be limited to the big event, but should be available for a Tuesday night date any time of the year. If it is winter, when cranberries are in season and you happen to have some sauce on hand, use it. But other times, feel free to use canned whole-berry cranberry sauce, an excellent all-American product. We like this dish with steamed green beans, baked sweet potatoes, and spice cookies for dessert.

$1\frac{1}{4}$ pounds turkey breast cutlets, cut into 4 pieces
    Salt and freshly ground pepper
3 tablespoons butter
$\frac{2}{3}$ cup dry white wine
$\frac{2}{3}$ cup cooked whole-berry cranberry sauce
1 cup thinly sliced green onions
1 tablespoon chopped fresh sage
1 tablespoon chopped fresh thyme

Season the turkey with salt and pepper. In a large skillet, heat the butter. Sauté the turkey over medium-high heat, turning once, until golden and cooked through, about 8 minutes total. Transfer the turkey to a plate.

Add the wine to the pan drippings and cook for 2 minutes, stirring up any browned bits on the bottom of the pan. Stir in the cranberry sauce, green onions, sage, and thyme. Reduce the heat to medium-low and simmer, stirring often, until slightly reduced, 2 to 4 minutes. Season to taste with salt and pepper. Return the turkey and accumulated juices to the pan and simmer until the turkey is heated through, about 1 minute.

pork

Like chicken, pork has really come of age in the past couple of decades. It was once designated the fattiest and least healthy of meats, and pork producers responded on a couple of fronts. First, they started breeding much, much leaner hogs, and then, in a brilliant public relations gambit, officially designated pork as "the other white meat." Second, they developed different butchering techniques, which have resulted in many nifty new and more versatile cuts, particularly boneless varieties such as tenderloins, cutlets, and boneless chops, all of which should be cooked quickly to ensure maximum flavor and tenderness. The only downside to this leaner pork for the cook is that she has to make sure it stays juicy as it cooks and does not dry out.

We've learned that top-of-the-stove cooking is especially appropriate for pork, because a sharp eye can guard against overcooking the meat (which is harder to do if it's in the oven). So in this chapter, we give you plenty of recipes for chops, such as Braised Bay Leaf Pork Chops (page 52), Granny Smith's Pork Chops Braised with Leeks (page 51), Indoor Bourbon BBQ Pork with Thyme Onions (page 53), as well as recipes for sautéed medallions cut from the tenderloin, such as Bosc and Sage Pork Medallions (page 46). There are also a delicious mustardy braised tenderloin stew, a spicy stir-fried pork dish, and a couple of winning recipes for smoked ham steaks and Canadian bacon.

Succulent ground pork shows up in a quick version of posole with hominy, and those wonderfully juicy and flavorful pork sausages are showcased in such dishes as Tuscan Sausages and Cannellini Beans on Arugula (page 59) and Kielbasa and Potato Skillet Dinner (page 61).

recipes

fennel-crusted
pork chops
and charred lemons *4 servings*

Aromatic fennel seeds form a pleasing, slightly licorice-flavored crust on this boneless pork chop sauté; cooking the lemon slices softens and mellows their sharp flavor. The result is a dish that is deliciously exotic and yet very, very quick and easy. Good accompaniments would be cumin-spiced couscous or one of the many flavored couscous mixes on the market, along with steamed baby carrots that have been tossed with butter and chopped fresh mint. Finish with a plate of purchased pastries, such as baklava.

- 1 tablespoon fennel seeds
- 4 center-cut boneless pork chops, about 1 inch thick
  Salt and freshly ground pepper
- 4 tablespoons olive oil
- 2 lemons
- 3 garlic cloves, finely chopped
- 1 cup chicken broth
- 2 tablespoons chopped parsley

Place the fennel seeds in a sturdy plastic bag and use a mallet or rolling pin to roughly crush the seeds. Season the pork chops with salt and pepper and sprinkle with the fennel seeds, pressing them into the surface of the meat.

In a large skillet, heat 2 tablespoons of the oil. Cook the pork chops over medium heat until well browned on both sides and almost completely cooked within, regulating the heat so the seeds don't burn, about 8 minutes. Transfer to a plate, leaving the drippings in the pan.

While the pork is cooking, cut one of the lemons into thin slices, remove the seeds, and set aside. Squeeze 2 tablespoons of juice from the remaining lemon and reserve.

Add the remaining 2 tablespoons of oil to the skillet. Add the lemon slices and cook over medium heat until well browned and caramelized, about 2 minutes. Remove to the plate with the pork. Add the garlic to the pan drippings and cook, stirring, just until fragrant, about 30 seconds. Add the broth and reserved lemon juice, raise the heat to high, and bring to a boil. Cook, stirring up any browned bits clinging to the bottom of the pan, until the liquid is reduced by about one third, 2 to 3 minutes. Return the pork, lemons, and any accumulated juices to the pan, and simmer over medium heat until the pork is cooked through and no trace of pink remains, 2 to 3 minutes. Season to taste with salt and pepper. (The pork can be cooked up to 1 hour ahead and set aside at cool room temperature. Reheat gently.)

Stir in the parsley and serve.

bosc and sage pork medallions *4 servings*

Buttery, tender pork tenderloin can be easily sliced and flattened with the palm of the hand into thin medallions, which make a fabulous sauté. Here, the sweet-and-sour pan sauce is made by caramelizing sliced pears and tossing in a good handful of sage. The spicy Bosc is our favorite pear for most cooking, both for its flavor and because its firm texture holds up well. Buttered and parslied egg noodles and steamed Swiss chard would be excellent accompaniments, and lemon pie or lemon bars would complete the meal nicely.

1 large or 2 small pork tenderloins (1¼ to 1½ pounds total)
⅓ cup flour
4 tablespoons chopped fresh sage, plus sprigs for garnish
Salt and freshly ground pepper
3 tablespoons olive oil
2 tablespoons butter
1 large, firm Bosc pear, cored, peeled, and thinly sliced
3 garlic cloves, finely chopped
1½ cups chicken broth
3 tablespoons red wine vinegar

Slice the tenderloins crosswise into rounds ½ inch thick. Place between two sheets of plastic wrap and use the palm of your hand or a rolling pin to flatten into medallions about ¼ inch thick. On a plate, stir together the flour and 2 tablespoons of the sage. Season the pork with salt and pepper and then dredge in the flour, shaking off any excess.

In a large skillet, heat the oil. Add the meat and cook over medium heat until nicely browned on both sides and cooked through, 3 to 5 minutes total. Transfer to a plate, leaving the drippings in the pan.

Add the butter to the skillet, then add the pear and cook, stirring frequently, until it begins to soften and brown, about 2 minutes. Add the garlic and cook, stirring, for 1 minute. Add the broth and bring to a boil, stirring up any brown bits in the bottom of the pan. Boil until the sauce is slightly reduced and thickened, about 2 minutes. Add the vinegar and stir in the remaining 2 tablespoons of sage. Return the meat and any accumulated juices to the pan and simmer just until heated through. Season to taste with salt and pepper. (The pork can be cooked up to 1 hour ahead and held at cool room temperature or refrigerated. Reheat gently.)

pork schnitzel with a lemon spritz

4 servings

Now that pork comes in all kinds of nifty cuts, we enjoy creating dishes that showcase each to its best effect, including this schnitzel recipe designed for boneless pork cutlets. It's a wonderful any-night-of-the-week kind of main course. For family fare, just add some frozen au gratin potatoes and a sliced tomato salad to each plate. If you are making the schnitzel for guests, take some time to make your own scalloped potatoes (include a handful of chopped fresh herbs), and add some steamed *haricots verts* to the menu. A bakery-made strudel—either cherry, apple, or pear—would be the perfect finish.

2 large lemons
3 slices good-quality white bread
¼ cup all-purpose flour
1 teaspoon salt
½ teaspoon pepper
1 large egg
1¼ pounds pork cutlets
2 tablespoons butter
1 tablespoon light olive oil

Grate 1 teaspoon of zest from one of the lemons. Cut the lemons into a total of 8 wedges. Tear the bread into pieces and whir in a food processor to make about 1¼ cups of fine crumbs. Spread out onto a plate. On another plate, stir the flour together with the lemon zest, salt, and pepper. In a shallow dish, whisk the egg with 1 tablespoon of water.

Place the cutlets between two sheets of plastic wrap and with a heavy skillet, flat mallet, or rolling pin, pound the meat to a thickness of about ¼ inch. Cut the meat into smaller pieces if necessary to fit into the pan. Dredge the cutlets in the seasoned flour, shaking off the excess; then dip in the egg, and finally, dredge in the crumbs, patting them on to coat completely. (The cutlets may be breaded several hours ahead and refrigerated.)

In a large skillet, heat the butter and oil. Cook the pork over medium to medium-high heat, in two batches if necessary, turning once, until the cutlets are golden brown on both sides and no longer pink within, about 6 minutes per batch. Serve with the lemon wedges for spritzing the schnitzels at the table.

cumin-crusted pork paillards with mojo pan sauce *4 servings*

Mojo is the ubiquitous table sauce of Cuba, similar to a vinaigrette, except that in a mojo sauce the garlic is always cooked a bit to mellow and deepen its flavor. In this sauté, thinly sliced pork cutlets are pounded even thinner to make paillards, and then dusted in cumin-seasoned flour, echoing the cumin in the sauce. Offer side dishes of yellow rice pilaf (tinted with turmeric) and seasoned black beans. Finish with pineapple slices sprinkled with brown sugar and run under the broiler to caramelize the sugar.

1¼ pounds pork cutlets
¼ cup all-purpose flour
1 tablespoon plus 2 teaspoons ground cumin
1 teaspoon salt
1 teaspoon pepper
¼ cup plus 2 tablespoons olive oil
3 large garlic cloves, finely chopped
⅓ cup fresh orange juice
⅓ cup fresh lemon juice
2 tablespoons chopped parsley
Orange wedges for garnish

Place the meat between two sheets of plastic wrap and with a heavy skillet, meat mallet, or rolling pin, pound to a thickness of about ¼ inch. Cut the meat into smaller pieces, if necessary, to fit into the pan. On a plate, combine the flour and 1 tablespoon plus 1 teaspoon of the cumin with the salt and pepper. Dredge the pork in the seasoned flour, shaking off any excess.

In a large skillet, heat 2 tablespoons of the oil. Cook the pork over medium heat, in two batches if necessary, turning once, until well browned on both sides and no longer pink within, about 6 minutes per batch. Transfer to a warm platter, leaving the drippings in the pan.

Add the remaining ¼ cup of oil to the skillet. Add the garlic and cook over medium heat, stirring, until just barely tinged with gold, about 1 minute. Remove the pan from the heat and add the orange and lemon juices. Return the pan to the stove, raise the heat to high, bring to a boil, and cook the sauce for 30 seconds. Stir in the parsley and season to taste with salt and pepper. Serve the pork with the sauce spooned over it, garnished with the orange wedges.

pork, hominy, and fresh chile posole *4 servings*

This is a delightfully shortened, quickened, and light-ened version of posole, a long-simmered pork and hominy stew, which originated in Jalisco, on Mexico's Pacific Coast. Traditional accompaniments—shredded lettuce, sliced radishes, green onions—are served in small bowls at the table for adding to the stew, or you can combine them into a chopped salad dressed with a light vinaigrette. A basket of warm tortillas, either corn or flour, and brownies topped with cinnamon ice cream would round out this meal to perfection. By the way, in case you're not familiar with hominy (soft, lye-soaked corn kernels), look for it in cans on the same shelf as canned beans or in the Mexican section of your supermarket.

¼ cup light olive oil
1 pound lean ground pork
1 large onion, coarsely chopped
1 tablespoon plus 1 teaspoon ground cumin
2 tablespoons all-purpose flour
4 cups chicken broth
3 cups golden hominy, rinsed and drained
2 tablespoons finely chopped jalapeño peppers, or to taste
¾ cup chopped cilantro, plus sprigs for garnish
Salt and freshly ground pepper

In a large, deep skillet, heat the oil. Add the pork, onion, and cumin, and cook over medium-high heat, stirring frequently, until the meat is brown, about 5 minutes. Add the flour and cook, stirring, for 2 min-utes. Whisk in the broth and add the hominy. Bring to a boil, stirring until the sauce is smooth and bubbly. Reduce the heat to medium and simmer, uncovered, stirring occasionally, until thickened, 15 to 20 minutes. (The posole can be made to this point up to 1 day ahead and refrigerated. Reheat gently.)

Stir in the jalapeños and cilantro and simmer for a few minutes to blend the flavors. Season to taste with salt and pepper. Ladle into shallow bowls and garnish with cilantro sprigs.

granny smith's pork chops braised with leeks

4 servings

This is a wonderful braised pork recipe, simple yet sophisticated, with lots of flavorful juices, so you'll need to serve it with something like mashed white or sweet potatoes on the side. Brussels sprouts with brown butter or another green vegetable would be a good choice. Then, complete the meal with a homey dessert such as squares of gingerbread or another spice cake topped with cinnamon-scented whipped cream.

3 tablespoons butter

4 center-cut, bone-in pork chops, about 1 inch thick
  Salt and freshly ground pepper

3 large leeks, thinly sliced (white and pale green parts only)

1 large Granny Smith or other tart apple, cored and thinly sliced

1 tablespoon all-purpose flour

1 cup chicken broth

½ cup dry white wine

In a large skillet with a lid, heat 1 tablespoon of the butter. Season the pork chops well on both sides with salt and pepper and cook over medium-high heat until well browned on both sides, about 6 minutes total. Transfer to a plate, leaving the drippings in the pan.

Add the remaining 2 tablespoons of butter to the pan. Add the leeks and cook, stirring frequently, until they begin to soften, about 5 minutes. Add the apple and cook, stirring, until the fruit begins to brown, about 2 minutes. Add the flour and cook, stirring, for 1 minute. Add the broth and wine and bring to a boil, whisking until the sauce is bubbly.

Return the pork chops and any accumulated juices to the skillet and simmer, covered, until the pork is tender and cooked through, about 10 minutes. Season to taste with salt and pepper. (The pork chops can be cooked a couple of hours ahead and held at cool room temperature or refrigerated. Reheat gently.)

braised
bay leaf
pork chops *4 servings*

We've discovered that lightly browning bay leaves helps release their aromatic perfume, giving a flavor boost to quickly cooked braises such as this one. Caramelizing—in this case, heaps of sliced onions—also deepens flavor and enhances the color of this wonderful autumnal dish. Partner the savory pork chops with boiled parslied potatoes and steamed Swiss chard or collards, and may we suggest warm ginger-bread topped with dollops of lemon curd for dessert?

4 center-cut, boneless or bone-in pork chops, about 1 inch thick
  Salt and freshly ground pepper
2 tablespoons chopped fresh sage, plus sprigs for garnish
3 tablespoons light olive oil
2 bay leaves
2 large onions, thinly sliced
½ cup thinly sliced celery
1½ cups chicken broth
1 tablespoon cider vinegar

Season the pork chops well with salt and pepper and sprinkle on both sides with about half the sage, pressing it into the meat. In a large skillet with a lid, heat 2 tablespoons of the oil. Cook the pork chops and the bay leaves over medium-high heat until the meat is well browned on both sides and the bay leaves are lightly browned, about 6 minutes. Transfer both the meat and the bay leaves to a plate, leaving the drippings in the pan.

Add the remaining 1 tablespoon of oil to the skillet. Add the onions and celery and cook, stirring frequently, until the vegetables are nicely browned and begin to soften, about 5 minutes. Add the broth, raise the heat to high, and bring to a boil, stirring up any browned bits on the bottom of the pan. Return the pork chops and any accumulated juices to the skillet, along with the bay leaves, and add the remaining sage. Bring to a boil, cover, reduce the heat to medium-low, and simmer until the pork is tender and cooked through, about 10 minutes. Stir in the vinegar. If there is too much liquid, cook, uncovered, to reduce the juices slightly before serving. (The pork chops can be cooked up to several hours ahead and refrigerated. Reheat gently.)

Season to taste with salt and pepper, remove the bay leaves, and garnish with sage sprigs before serving.

indoor bourbon
bbq pork with
thyme onions *4 servings*

We turn to this indoor pork barbecue in the dead of winter, when even intrepid grill mistresses like ourselves aren't quite willing to venture out into the gale to fire up the barbie. A truism that applies to all bottled condiments: when perusing the supermarket shelves for barbecue sauce, be sure to buy the best quality available (which often correlates directly with the highest sticker price). Add baked white or sweet potatoes, a side of purchased coleslaw, and some corn muffins, and you've got yourself a downright divine country supper.

    4 tablespoons light olive oil or vegetable oil
    2 medium onions, thinly sliced
    2 tablespoons cider vinegar
    2 tablespoons chopped fresh thyme
 1¼ pounds thinly sliced boneless pork chops
       Freshly ground pepper
    ¾ cup good-quality bottled barbecue sauce
    3 tablespoons bourbon

In a large skillet, heat 2 tablespoons of the oil. Add the onions and cook over medium to medium-high heat, stirring occasionally, until they are softened and tinged with some black edges, 10 to 15 minutes. Add the vinegar and 1 tablespoon of the thyme and cook over high heat, stirring, until the vinegar evaporates, about 2 minutes. Transfer the onions to a plate. Do not wash the pan.

Add the remaining 2 tablespoons of oil to the skillet. Season the pork chops generously with pepper and cook them over medium to medium-high heat until nicely browned on both sides, about 5 minutes. Add the barbecue sauce, bourbon, remaining tablespoon of thyme, and ½ cup of water. Cook, stirring and scraping the bottom of the pan, until the sauce comes to a boil and is bubbly. Simmer, uncovered, over medium heat until the sauce is slightly thickened and the pork is no longer pink inside, about 5 minutes. (The pork chops can be made up to several hours ahead and refrigerated. Reheat the pork and onions gently.)

Serve the pork and sauce with the thyme onions spooned over the top.

mustard pork and root vegetable braise

4 servings

It wouldn't occur to many people to braise a pork tenderloin, but we've discovered that it actually takes beautifully to this method of cooking with moist heat. And since the tenderloin is a very lean cut, it doesn't need long simmering to tenderize it. Great accompaniments to this savory "pot roast" would be mashed potatoes topped with some snipped chives, a chicory and orange salad, and a basket of seeded pumpernickel bread or rolls. Chocolate or butterscotch pudding topped with Kahlua whipped cream would be the perfect ending.

1 large or 2 small pork tenderloins (1¼ to 1½ pounds total), each cut in half crosswise
Salt and freshly ground pepper
3 tablespoons chopped fresh thyme, plus whole sprigs for garnish
3 tablespoons olive oil
3 parsnips, peeled and cut into 1-inch pieces
2½ cups peeled baby carrots (10 ounces)
1½ cups frozen pearl onions
½ teaspoon sugar
1¾ cups chicken broth
2 tablespoons coarse-grain Dijon mustard

Season the pork on all sides with salt and pepper and press about half the thyme into the surface of the meat. In a large, deep skillet with a lid, heat the oil. Add the pork and cook over medium-high heat until browned well on all sides, about 5 minutes total. Remove to a plate, leaving the drippings in the pan.

Add the parsnips, carrots, and onions to the skillet and sprinkle with the sugar. Cook over medium heat, stirring occasionally, until the vegetables begin to caramelize and soften, 3 to 5 minutes. Add the broth and remaining thyme, and return the meat and any accumulated juices to the pan. Simmer, covered, over medium-low heat until the vegetables are tender and the pork is no longer pink in the center, about 20 minutes.

Transfer the pork to a platter. Whisk the mustard into the sauce to distribute it evenly, and season to taste with salt and pepper. (The dish can be made up to several hours ahead and refrigerated. Reheat gently.)

When ready to serve, cut the pork on the diagonal into ¾-inch slices and arrange on a platter. Spoon the sauce and vegetables over the meat and garnish with thyme sprigs.

peppery pork, peanut, and watercress stir-fry *4 servings*

Since the actual cooking happens in a matter of mere seconds, the trick to executing any stir-fry is to have all the elements chopped and at the ready before you begin, preferably lined up in a row in the order of their use. This stir-fry has the zing of heat from a pepper spice blend (McCormick's makes a couple, including one called Szechuan Blend), balanced by the sweetness of honey-roasted peanuts and the fresh tang of bitter greens. Serve it with steamed white rice (make sure it's ready before you begin stir-frying), a cooling cucumber and yogurt salad, and fresh figs or chilled grapes, with a plate of spice cookies for dessert.

1¼ pounds boneless pork chops or pork tenderloin, trimmed of any external fat

1 tablespoon mixed pepper seasoning, such as Szechuan pepper mix

3 tablespoons peanut or vegetable oil

3 cloves garlic, finely chopped

2 large bunches or two 4-ounce bags watercress, thickest stems removed

⅔ cup chicken broth

2 tablespoons soy sauce

⅓ cup honey-roasted peanuts

Cut the pork crosswise into thin strips. (If using tenderloin, first cut into ½-inch-thick slices. It is easiest to do this if the meat is partially frozen.) Sprinkle the pork strips with the pepper seasoning, tossing to coat.

In a large, heavy skillet, heat 2 tablespoons of the oil over high heat. Add the pork and cook, undisturbed, until it begins to blacken a bit on the bottom, 1 to 2 minutes. Stir and cook 1 more minute until the meat is no longer pink inside. Using a slotted spoon, remove the strips to a plate.

Reduce the heat to medium-high and add the remaining tablespoon of oil to the pan. Add the garlic and half the watercress and cook, turning with tongs, until the watercress begins to wilt; then add the remaining watercress. Cook, turning, about 1 minute. Return the pork and any accumulated juices to the pan, add the broth and soy sauce, and simmer for 1 minute to blend the flavors. Sprinkle with the peanuts before serving.

italian
sausages and
broccoli rabe *4 servings*

Packaged instant polenta or sliced and heated polenta roll is the ideal partner to this hearty main course. You might begin the meal with a selection of deli antipasto (olives, roasted peppers, and other vegetables), and finish with sliced and sugared strawberries spooned over ricotta cheesecake.

1¼ pounds sweet Italian sausages, cut into 3-inch
     lengths if in one long link
½ cup dry white wine
3 tablespoons fruity olive oil
3 large garlic cloves, finely chopped
1 large bunch broccoli rabe, trimmed
1 cup chicken broth
⅓ cup freshly grated Parmesan cheese

Put the sausages in a large skillet with a lid. Prick the sausages in a few places with a fork, add the wine, and bring to a boil. Cover the pan, reduce the heat to medium-low, and cook for 5 minutes. Uncover, raise the heat to medium to medium-high, and cook until browned and cooked through, 8 to 10 minutes. Transfer to a plate, leaving the drippings in the pan.

Pour off all but 2 tablespoons of the pan drippings and add the oil. Add the garlic and cook over medium heat, stirring, for 30 seconds. Add the broccoli rabe, broth, and ½ cup of water. Bring to a boil, stirring up any browned bits in the bottom of the pan. Reduce the heat to medium-low and simmer, covered, until the broccoli rabe is almost tender, about 10 minutes. Return the sausages to the pan and heat through.

Spoon the sausages and broccoli rabe onto plates and pass the cheese separately.

tuscan sausages
and cannellini beans
on arugula *4 servings*

Tuscans are very fond of beans and sausages. Here
we combine the two in a simplified takeoff on a traditional Italian recipe. The beans simmer for a few
minutes in a white wine bath, imbibing a good
amount of winy flavor as they steep, and then the
mélange is served on a bed of peppery fresh arugula
leaves. Complete this all-in-one-pot supper with some
seeded semolina bread and an easy dessert—maybe
figs filled with mascarpone cheese.

1¼ pounds hot Italian sausages, cut in half lengthwise
1½ cups dry white wine
  2 tablespoons fruity olive oil
  1 large onion, chopped
  1 large red bell pepper, chopped
  ¼ cup chopped fresh oregano or marjoram
  3 cups drained canned cannellini or other white
       beans
  2 bunches or two 4-ounce bags arugula

Put the sausages in a large, deep skillet with a lid.
Prick each sausage in a few places with a fork, add
¼ cup of the wine, and bring to a boil over high heat.
Reduce the heat to medium-low and cook, covered,
for 5 minutes. Uncover, raise the heat to medium-
high, and cook, turning occasionally, until the
sausages are brown and cooked through, 8 to 10 minutes. Transfer to a plate and slice thinly on the
diagonal.

Pour off all but 2 tablespoons of the drippings
from the skillet and add the oil. Add the onion and
bell pepper and cook over medium heat until the
vegetables are softened and beginning to brown, about
8 minutes. Stir in the oregano. Add the beans and the
remaining 1¼ cups of wine and bring to a boil, stirring up any browned bits in the bottom of the pan.
Reduce the heat to medium and simmer, uncovered,
for about 5 minutes, until most of the wine is
absorbed. Add the sausages and heat through. (The
dish can be cooked up to several hours ahead and
refrigerated. Reheat gently.)

To serve, spoon the sausage mixture over the
arugula.

choucroute garni with sausages *4 servings*

In the classic, elaborate, long-cooked Alsatian choucroute, several smoked meats are the rule, including
bacon and sometimes ham. Here we suggest using
cooked sausages alone. There are so many excellent
ones available these days. Old-fashioned German
sausages (brats and knocks) are wonderful, but you
could also use any of the new flavors, such as sausages
seasoned with apple or herbs. Parslied, boiled red-
skinned potatoes and a spinach salad tossed with citrus
vinaigrette are good accompaniments. Finish with
warm apple strudel, topped with vanilla ice cream.

1¼ pounds cooked pork or mixed-meat sausages,
      such as bratwurst or knockwurst
  3 tablespoons light olive oil
  1 large onion, coarsely chopped
1½ teaspoons caraway seeds
  1 large bay leaf, broken in half
  1 pound sauerkraut, rinsed and drained
  ¾ cup dry white wine
      Freshly ground pepper

Cut each sausage in half lengthwise. Heat the oil in a
large skillet with a lid. Add the sausages, cut-sides
down, and cook over medium-high heat until nicely
browned, 3 to 4 minutes. Turn the sausages, add the
onion, and cook over medium heat, stirring frequently, until the onion is golden and the sausage is
browned on the other side, about 5 minutes.

Stir in the caraway seeds, bay leaf, sauerkraut, and
wine. Bring to a boil, reduce the heat to medium-low,
and simmer, covered, for 10 minutes to blend the flavors. If there is too much liquid in the sauerkraut,
cook, uncovered, for a few minutes to reduce and
thicken. (The choucroute can be made up to 2 hours
ahead and set aside at cool room temperature or refrigerated. Reheat gently.)

Season well with pepper and remove the pieces of
bay leaf before serving.

kielbasa and potato skillet dinner

4 servings

In this recipe, kielbasa, that decidedly garlicky smoked Polish sausage, is thinly sliced, browned, and simmered with potatoes in an aromatic apple-and-wine-flavored liquid to create a wonderfully warming, all-in-one-skillet dinner. All you need to add are steamed broccoli spears, a basket of seeded rye bread, and perhaps a slice of spice layer cake for dessert.

2 tablespoons olive oil

¾ pound kielbasa, cut into ¼-inch-thick slices

1 large onion, sliced

2 pounds all-purpose potatoes, peeled and thinly sliced (5 to 6 cups)

2 tablespoons all-purpose flour

3 tablespoons chopped fresh thyme, or 2 teaspoons dried

½ teaspoon freshly ground pepper

1 cup apple juice or apple cider

½ cup dry white wine

1 bay leaf, broken in half

Salt (optional)

In a large, deep skillet with a lid, heat the oil. Add the kielbasa and onion and cook over medium heat, stirring frequently, until the onion is softened and the kielbasa begins to brown, about 5 minutes.

Add the potatoes, sprinkle with the flour, thyme, and pepper, and stir gently to combine. Pour the apple juice, wine, and 2 cups of water over the potato mixture and tuck the bay leaf into the liquid. Bring to a boil over high heat, reduce the heat to medium-low to low, and cook, covered, until the potatoes are tender and much of the liquid has been absorbed, about 25 minutes. Taste and season with pepper and salt, if necessary. No salt may be needed because the sausage is quite salty. (The dish can be made up to 1 hour ahead and held at cool room temperature or refrigerated. Reheat gently.)

Remove the bay leaf pieces before serving.

canadian bacon with red-eye cream *4 servings*

In its true Southern form, red-eye gravy is made by frying up some country ham and deglazing the pan with strong coffee. Here, cream is also added to smooth out the rough edges of the sauce. You can actually substitute just about any ham for the Canadian bacon in this recipe—ham steak or leftover baked ham would work beautifully. Complete this supper with purchased corn muffins or homemade cornbread and a salad of chicory or other bitter greens dressed with a honey-mustard vinaigrette. And to carry out the Southern theme, how about peach or pecan pie for dessert?

2 tablespoons butter
12 to 16 slices Canadian bacon (about 1 pound)
3 tablespoons brewed coffee (see Note)
⅔ cup heavy cream
1 tablespoon chopped parsley
¼ teaspoon freshly ground pepper
  Salt (optional)

In a large skillet, heat the butter. Add the Canadian bacon and cook over medium to medium-high heat, turning once, until the edges are tinged with dark brown, about 5 minutes total. Remove to a plate, leaving the drippings in the pan. Cover with foil to keep warm.

Add the coffee to the skillet and boil for a few seconds, stirring to dissolve any caramelized juices in the pan. Add the cream, bring to a boil, and simmer until the sauce is slightly reduced and thickened, about 3 minutes. Stir in the parsley and pepper. Taste, and add a small amount of salt, if necessary. (Since the ham is quite salty, no additional salt may be needed.) Spoon the red-eye cream over the Canadian bacon and serve.

note:
You can use strong brewed coffee or dissolve 2 teaspoons of instant coffee granules in 3 tablespoons of boiling water.

peppered ham steaks on vinegared greens

4 servings

Ham and greens are made for each other—one of those culinary marriages made in heaven. We use spinach here, but the recipe would be equally good made with arugula or watercress, both of which you can also buy prewashed, in bags. Good accompaniments to this main dish are baked potatoes topped with a spoonful of soft herbed cheese, coarse-grain mustard, dill pickles, and maybe a slice of coconut custard pie for dessert.

1¼ pounds ham steaks, cut into 4 or 8 pieces
    Coarsely ground pepper
 4 tablespoons butter
 ½ cup chopped sweet onion, such as Vidalia or
    Spanish onion
Two 10-ounce bags baby spinach leaves
 2 tablespoons tarragon vinegar

Sprinkle the ham generously on both sides with the pepper. In a large skillet, heat 2 tablespoons of the butter. Cook the ham over medium heat until the edges are tinged with golden brown and the ham is heated through, about 8 minutes total. Remove to a warm plate, leaving any drippings in the pan.

Add the remaining 2 tablespoons of butter to the skillet. Add the onion and cook, stirring frequently, until they begin to soften, about 3 minutes. Raise the heat to high, add half the spinach to the pan, and cook, turning with tongs, until it begins to wilt. Add the rest of the spinach and continue to cook, turning, until the spinach wilts and softens, 2 to 3 minutes more. Add the vinegar and toss to combine.

To serve, place the spinach on plates or a platter and arrange the ham around it.

beef

It's such an old joke by now, but the "Where's the beef?" line still resonates in this country. True, beef has taken its share of knocks in recent years, but when you get right down to it, we're still a nation that loves its well-marbled steaks and juicy burgers, and a week's worth of menus seems somehow deficient if it doesn't include at least one beef main course.

These days, beef can be turned into so much more than the plain, unadorned slabs of meat of yore, and skillet cookery is an excellent way to begin and end the process. Pan searing, sometimes called pan grilling, turns out to be the ideal cooking method for small, boneless, relatively thin (not more than about an inch thick) beef steaks. So we offer two admirable recipes that use this technique—Peppered Filets Mignons with Brandy and Blue Cheese (page 68), and Pan-Seared Tenderloin Steaks with Sherried Mushroom Sauce (page 66). Pan searing is also perfect for cooking cubed steaks, thinly sliced "sandwich steaks," and, of course, beef stir-fries.

Ground beef is the stuff of beloved comfort food dishes such as meatballs and chili, but our recipes often go one better by tweaking some of these old standards with updated techniques and unusual seasonings. Meatballs Basilico (page 76) is lifted from the humdrum to the sublime by the simple addition of a large handful of pungently fragrant fresh basil to both meatballs and sauce. Chipotle chiles in adobo enliven the chili (page 77), Our Picadillo (page 80) is enhanced by the surprising complexity of pumpkin pie spice mix, and Asian peanut sauce adds depth and interest to Thai-Style Beef and Lettuce Wraps (page 78).

So, here's the beef!

recipes

pan-seared tenderloin steaks with sherried mushroom sauce *4 servings*

Cut from the beef tenderloin (and sometimes called tournedos), these boneless steaks are lean and as tender as butter. Tenderloin steaks are the perfect foil for an enhancing sauce, and mushrooms are a wonderful complement to beef. These days fresh mushrooms—for example, cremini, portobello, and shiitake—come packaged conveniently mixed together in ten-ounce boxes in the produce section, so use one of those mixtures or, if you have a favorite among them, simply use a single type of wild mushroom. They'll all work beautifully. This special entrée deserves equally special accompaniments, such as buttered baby carrots sprinkled with chopped chervil, twice-baked potatoes, and a watercress salad topped with crumbled Roquefort. Lemon mousse cake or tiramisu would be a fitting finish.

  1 tablespoon light olive oil
  4 beef tenderloin steaks (tournedos), 1 inch thick
      Salt and freshly ground pepper
  4 tablespoons chilled butter
 10 ounces fresh wild and/or cultivated mushrooms,
      such as cremini, portobello, or shiitake,
      tough stems removed and coarsely chopped
  3 tablespoons chopped shallots
  1 cup dry sherry
  2 tablespoons chopped fresh thyme, plus sprigs
      for garnish

In a large skillet, heat the olive oil. Sprinkle the steaks generously with salt and pepper. Add the steaks to the pan and cook over medium-high heat until nicely browned on the outside and cooked to the desired degree of doneness within, about 3 minutes per side for medium-rare. (Be especially careful not to overcook.) Transfer the steaks to a plate, leaving any drippings in the pan. Tent the steaks with foil or keep warm in a very low oven while making the sauce.

Add 2 tablespoons of the butter to the skillet. Add the mushrooms and shallots and cook over medium to medium-high heat, stirring frequently, until the mushrooms give up their liquid and begin to brown, about 5 minutes. Add the sherry and thyme and boil until the liquid is reduced by half, about 3 minutes.

Cut the remaining 2 tablespoons of butter into several pieces. Add the butter to the sauce, a couple of pieces at a time, whisking as it melts. Season to taste with salt and pepper.

Spoon the sauce over the steaks, garnish with thyme sprigs, and serve.

peppered filets mignons with brandy and blue cheese

4 servings

Trends come and go, but tender filet mignon beef-steaks have endured as nearly everyone's pick for the ultimate in special meat treats. Fortunately, they are also among the quickest cuts to prepare. They take especially well to pan grilling and in less than fifteen minutes, you can have an extraordinarily elegant entrée. Great accompaniments would be roasted garlic-rosemary new potatoes, steamed asparagus spears, and perhaps wedges of chocolate mousse cake drizzled with chocolate ganache for dessert.

2 tablespoons butter
4 filet mignon steaks, about 1 inch thick
  Salt
2 to 3 teaspoons cracked black peppercorns
1 cup beef broth
½ cup brandy or cognac
1 cup crumbled blue cheese

In a large skillet, heat the butter. Season the steaks with salt and pat the pepper firmly onto both sides. Add the steaks to the skillet and cook over medium-high heat until nicely browned on the outside and cooked to the desired degree of doneness within, about 3 minutes per side for medium-rare. Transfer the steaks to a plate, leaving the drippings in the pan.

Add the broth and brandy to the skillet, raise the heat to high, and boil, scraping up any browned bits from the bottom of the pan, until the sauce is syrupy and reduced to about ⅔ cup, 3 to 5 minutes.

Spoon the sauce over the meat, top each steak with the crumbled blue cheese, and serve.

beef paillards
with mustard-anchovy jus
on arugula *4 servings*

Many chefs think of anchovies as their own little well-kept secret, especially when they are mashed and melted into a sauce, as they are here, and hence are invisible to the eye. Their intense, concentrated flavor somehow enhances without delivering any overpoweringly fishy notes at all. Paillards, which are essentially thinly sliced scallops, make for a sophisticated main course and call for equally interesting side dishes, such as one of the good couscous pilaf mixes now available, along with some skinny *haricots verts* tossed with butter and cherry or grape tomatoes. Baked pears topped with a dollop of crème fraîche would be a lovely dessert.

4 thinly sliced boneless rib-eye or other
   well-marbled steaks (about 5 ounces each)
   Salt and freshly ground pepper
3 tablespoons olive oil
⅓ cup chopped shallots
4 anchovies, chopped
3 tablespoons red wine vinegar
1 tablespoon coarse-grain mustard
1 tablespoon butter, cut into small pieces
1 large bunch (or 2 smaller bunches) arugula

Place the steaks between two sheets of plastic wrap and with a heavy skillet, meat mallet, or rolling pin, pound the meat to a thickness of approximately ¼ inch. Cut the paillards into 3- to 4-inch pieces and season on both sides with salt and pepper.

In a large skillet, heat the oil. Cook the steaks over medium-high heat (in two batches if necessary), until seared and well browned, less than 2 minutes per side for medium-rare. Transfer to a platter, leaving the drippings in the pan.

Add the shallots and anchovies to the pan drippings and cook, stirring and mashing the anchovies with the back of a spoon, for 2 minutes. Add the vinegar, bring to a boil, and whisk in the mustard. Remove the pan from the heat and whisk in the butter, one piece at a time, to make a smooth sauce.

Make a bed of arugula on serving plates or a platter, arrange the meat and any accumulated juices over the greens, and spoon the pan sauce over the meat.

skillet steak pizzaiola *4 servings*

According to our research, the concept of steak pizzaiola probably originated in Naples, but was quickly appropriated by Italian-American restaurateurs and became a menu staple during the mid-twentieth century. While you can't go wrong with the tomato-garlic-green pepper sauce, we've always thought it was sort of silly to put it over an expensive cut of steak. So we kept the pizzaiola, lost the pricey meat, and converted the dish into a more homey supper entrée by using cube steaks—and with delicious results. The sauce cries out for coarsely mashed potatoes, and braised escarole or broccoli rabe would be a good side vegetable choice.

3 tablespoons all-purpose flour
3 teaspoons Italian herb seasoning blend
1 teaspoon salt
1 teaspoon pepper
1¼ pounds cube steaks, cut into 4 equal pieces
¼ cup fruity olive oil
1 small green bell pepper, chopped
2 large garlic cloves, finely chopped
One 14½-ounce can Italian-style diced tomatoes
½ cup dry red wine

In a shallow dish, combine the flour, 2 teaspoons of the Italian herb seasoning, salt, and pepper. Dredge the steaks in the seasoned flour, shaking off the excess. Reserve any remaining flour mixture.

In a large skillet, heat the oil. Cook the steaks over medium-high to high heat until well crusted and browned on the outside, but still slightly pink within, about 2 minutes per side. Remove to a plate, leaving the drippings in the pan.

Add the bell pepper and garlic to the skillet and cook over medium-high heat, stirring almost constantly, for about 2 minutes. Add any reserved flour mixture and cook, stirring, for 1 minute. Add the tomatoes, wine, and ½ cup of water. Bring to a boil, reduce the heat to medium, and simmer, uncovered, for 5 to 8 minutes to reduce the sauce slightly and blend the flavors. Season to taste with salt and pepper. Place the meat atop the sauce and simmer until heated through. (The dish can be made up to 1 hour ahead and held at cool room temperature. Reheat gently.)

salt and pepper cube steaks with smoky red onion *4 servings*

We've been experimenting with some of the increasing numbers of spice blends on the market and have found many very much to our liking, including several of the blends of different peppers. Since these seasonings seem to go particularly well with beef, we put together this cube steak sauté. It couldn't be simpler, but the bold flavors of pepper, onion, and garlic are the perfect foil for the meat. This goes great with baked or oven-fried sweet potatoes and a big mixed green salad with blue cheese or ranch dressing. For dessert, how does butter pecan ice cream with chocolate sauce sound?

1¼ pounds cube steaks, cut into 4 equal pieces
    Salt
1 teaspoon pepper blend or ½ teaspoon each of black pepper and cayenne pepper
3 tablespoons olive oil
1 large red onion, thinly sliced
2 garlic cloves, finely chopped
½ cup dry red wine
2 teaspoons Dijon mustard

Season the steaks well with salt and sprinkle with the pepper, pressing so it adheres to the surface of the meat.

In a large skillet, heat 2 tablespoons of the oil. Cook the steaks over medium-high to high heat until well browned on both sides and still slightly pink within, about 2 minutes per side. Transfer to a plate, leaving the drippings in the pan.

Add the remaining tablespoon of oil to the pan. Add the onion and cook over medium to medium-high heat, stirring frequently, until it softens and the edges are brown, about 8 minutes. Add the garlic and cook, stirring, for 1 minute. Add the wine and ½ cup of water, raise the heat to high, and boil, scraping up any browned bits in the bottom of the pan, until the liquid is slightly reduced, about 1 minute. Stir in the mustard.

Return the steaks and any accumulated juices to the pan and reheat briefly. Serve the steaks with the smoky onion spooned over the top.

lemongrass beef
on a bed of
basil and greens *4 servings*

Fresh lemongrass is pretty easy to find in most super-markets these days, but if it's not available, then the dried version is quite acceptable. It will impart a good hit of that exquisitely haunting, herbaceous fragrance. If you use fresh lemongrass, peel off any dry exterior leaves and then finely mince only the juicy bulb, avoiding any woody stems. Since the salad is incorpo-rated into this Pacific Rim–inspired stir-fry, all you would need to add is steamed jasmine or basmati rice, along with a dessert of mixed melons tossed with crys-tallized ginger, and a plate of crisp cookies.

1¼ pounds lean, tender boneless beef such as top
     sirloin, cut into thin strips
2 tablespoons minced fresh lemongrass (white part
    only) or 2 teaspoons dried
3 tablespoons Thai fish sauce
1 tablespoon soy sauce
1½ teaspoons sugar
3 garlic cloves, minced
  Freshly ground pepper
2 tablespoons peanut oil
One 4½-ounce package mixed greens
1 cup thinly sliced red onions
¾ cup torn basil leaves, plus sprigs for garnish
½ cup bottled Asian dressing or balsamic vinaigrette

In a large bowl, combine the beef, lemongrass, fish sauce, soy sauce, sugar, and garlic. Sprinkle generously with pepper. Use your hands to mix all the ingredi-ents together thoroughly, and set aside for 10 minutes.

In a large skillet, heat the oil over high heat. When the oil is hot, add the beef mixture. Cook, undisturbed, until the meat begins to blacken on the bottom, about 2 minutes. Stir and cook until the meat is browned on all sides, 1 to 2 minutes more. Remove from the heat.

In a large bowl, combine the greens, onions, and basil. Drizzle with most of the dressing, toss, and transfer to a platter or plates. Spoon the meat over the greens, drizzle with the remaining dressing, garnish with basil sprigs, and serve.

sesame-hoisin beef stir-fry *4 servings*

Sesame seeds add crunch to this stir-fry, broccoli and red pepper provide the color, and bottled hoisin sauce pulls it all together. Hoisin, which is made from fermented soybeans, chili, sugar, ginger, and garlic, is an excellent replacement for some of the usual stir-fry flavorings, and because it often contains flour or cornstarch, hoisin glazes and thickens the dish, too. Start cooking your rice or noodles first, as you should when serving any super-quick stir-fry. Then all you need to add is a little green salad for a most satisfying supper.

3 tablespoons sesame seeds, preferably toasted
1¼ pounds lean, tender boneless beef, such as top sirloin, thinly sliced
Salt and freshly ground pepper
¼ cup peanut or vegetable oil
2 cups thinly sliced red bell peppers
1 cup sliced onions
6 cups broccoli florets (about 1 pound)
¼ cup hoisin sauce
1 tablespoon sesame oil

Place the sesame seeds on a plate. Season the beef with salt and pepper, and dredge in the seeds.

In a large skillet, heat the oil over high heat. When the oil is hot, add the bell peppers, onions, and broccoli. Cook, undisturbed, until the vegetables begin to char a little on the bottom, about 2 minutes. Stir and cook 1 minute more. Add the sesame-coated meat and stir once or twice. Again, cook until the bottoms of the vegetables and meat begin to blacken a bit, about 2 minutes. Reduce the heat to medium.

Add the hoisin sauce and ½ cup of water. Cook, stirring, until the sauce is bubbly and glazes all the meat and vegetables. Stir in the sesame oil and season to taste with salt and pepper.

ground sirloin patties with red wine pan sauce *4 servings*

Of course we should have known all along that the French wouldn't leave something as good as a ground beef patty out of their repertoire. Known as *bifteck haché* in France, this is a sophisticated rendition of the humble hamburger, enlivened by the addition of some sautéed onion and fresh herbs, and finished the way the French know best, with wine and cream. Natural accompaniments are potatoes au gratin, lightly buttered steamed spinach, and a bakery-made fruit tart for dessert.

> 3 tablespoons butter
> 1 cup chopped onions
> 1¼ pounds ground sirloin
> 2 tablespoons chopped fresh thyme, plus sprigs for garnish
> 1 teaspoon salt
> ½ teaspoon pepper
> ¼ cup all-purpose flour
> 1½ cups dry red wine
> ½ cup heavy cream

In a large skillet, heat 1 tablespoon of the butter. Add the onions and cook over medium heat until wilted, about 5 minutes. Transfer to a large bowl. (Do not wash the pan.) Add the sirloin, thyme, salt, and pepper to the bowl and mix gently but thoroughly with your hands. Shape into four ¾-inch-thick patties. Dredge the patties in the flour, shaking off any excess.

In the same skillet, heat the remaining 2 table-spoons of butter. Add the patties and cook over medium-high heat until nicely browned on the outside and pink within, about 3 minutes per side. Transfer to a plate and pour off any excess fat in the skillet.

Add the wine and bring to a boil, scraping up any browned bits in the bottom of the pan. Boil until reduced by about half, about 2 minutes. Add the cream and continue boiling, whisking constantly, until the sauce is slightly thickened, about 2 minutes.

Season to taste with salt and pepper and pour over the patties. Garnish with thyme sprigs and serve.

meatballs
basilico *4 servings*

Is there anyone of any age who doesn't love meatballs? These are distinguished by the addition of a goodly amount of fragrant fresh basil, added to the meat and also to the simple wine and tomato pan sauce in which the meatballs simmer. Our families like them with side dishes of roasted potatoes or egg noodles and steamed broccoli—or you might consider stuffing them into crusty grinder rolls and just adding a green salad to the plate.

  1 to 1¼ pounds ground beef, preferably chuck
  ¼ cup fine dry bread crumbs
  3 tablespoons grated Pecorino Romano cheese
  1 large egg
  ¼ cup plus 2 tablespoons chopped fresh basil
  2 garlic cloves, finely chopped
  ½ teaspoon salt
  ½ teaspoon pepper
  2 tablespoons olive oil, preferably extra-virgin
One 14½-ounce can Italian-style diced tomatoes
  ½ cup dry white wine

In a large bowl, combine the beef, bread crumbs, cheese, egg, ¼ cup of the basil, garlic, salt, and pepper. Use your hands to combine the mixture gently but thoroughly and shape into 8 meatballs, each about 2½ inches in diameter.

In a large skillet with a lid, heat the oil. Add the meatballs and cook over medium heat until well browned all over, about 8 minutes. Push the meatballs to the side of the pan, add the tomatoes, wine, and remaining 2 tablespoons of basil, and bring to a boil, scraping up any browned bits in the bottom of the pan. Partially cover the pan and simmer over medium-low heat until the meatballs are cooked through, 5 to 10 minutes. Season to taste with salt and pepper. (The meatballs can be made up to several hours ahead and refrigerated. Reheat gently.)

smoky chipotle chili *4 servings*

Chipotle chiles usually come packed in a seasoned tomato sauce called adobo, and they're a natural for adding extra zing and a wonderfully intriguing depth of flavor to chili. The chipotles themselves are actually smoked jalapeño peppers, which (be forewarned) are super hot. Use the suggested range of one to two tablespoons of minced chipotles with adobo, according to your fondness for more or less searing heat. Our favorite chili accompaniments are a basket of hot cornbread squares and a romaine, orange, and red onion salad.

1¼ pounds ground beef or a combination of beef and pork
1 large onion, chopped
1 large green bell pepper, chopped
3 garlic cloves, finely chopped
2 tablespoons good quality chili powder
2 teaspoons dried oregano
1 teaspoon ground cumin
One 14- to 16-ounce can diced tomatoes, preferably Mexican style
One 14- to 16-ounce can red kidney beans, drained
One 14- to 16-ounce can beef broth
1 to 2 tablespoons finely chopped chipotles in adobo, with some of the adobo sauce
Salt and freshly ground pepper

In a large, deep skillet with a lid, cook the ground meat with the onion, bell pepper, and garlic over medium to medium-high heat, stirring frequently, until the meat loses its pink color and the vegetables are softened, 6 to 8 minutes. Add the chili powder, oregano, and cumin and cook, stirring, for 1 minute.

Add the tomatoes, beans, broth, and chipotles in adobo. Bring to a boil, reduce the heat to medium-low, and simmer, partially covered, for 15 minutes to blend the flavors. Adjust the consistency, if necessary, by adding a little water to thin the chili or simmering, uncovered, for a few minutes to thicken to a spoonable, stewlike consistency. Season to taste with salt and pepper. (The chili can be made up to 2 days ahead and refrigerated or frozen. Reheat gently.)

thai-style beef and lettuce wraps *4 servings*

This is an adaptation of one of the finalist recipes from a recent Beef Council cook-off, and it's surely a winner in our book! Everybody we've served these spicy lettuce wraps to (kids included) really loves the taste—and the concept. Perhaps part of the appeal is the hands-on fun of rolling the seasoned meat mixture into a soft lettuce leaf to create these cute, fat, cigar-shaped wraps. Just add some Asian noodles tossed with fresh cilantro or a deli noodle or rice salad, and the meal is complete.

- 1¼ pounds lean ground beef
- 1 large onion, chopped
- ½ cup Asian peanut sauce (see Note)
- 1 tablespoon soy sauce
- 1 medium cucumber, peeled, seeded, and chopped (about 1¼ cups)
- ½ cup torn mint leaves, plus sprigs for garnish
  Salt and freshly ground pepper
- 12 large Boston lettuce leaves

In a large skillet set over medium-high heat, cook the beef and onion, breaking up the meat into small clumps with the side of a spoon, until the meat browns and the onion softens, about 8 minutes. Spoon off any excess fat. Add the peanut sauce, soy sauce, cucumber, and mint, and stir well to combine. Season to taste with salt and pepper.

Spoon some of the beef mixture into a lettuce leaf, fold in the sides, roll up, and garnish each wrap with a mint sprig. (Or, pass the ingredients for the wraps and let each person make her own.)

note:
There are several Asian peanut sauces on the market, but we think that Thai Kitchens brand is an especially good one.

our
picadillo *4 servings*

The literal translation for the Spanish picadillo is "hash," but the dish has evolved in Central America and the Caribbean into a kind of spicy ground meat stew. Usually the ingredients list is as long as your arm, but the pumpkin pie spice that we use here—a mix of cinnamon, nutmeg, allspice, and cloves—takes care of all the sweet spices usually called for. Picadillo makes a wonderful party dish for an informal get-together. Good accompaniments are steamed yellow rice from a mix (or make your own rice and tint it with turmeric or saffron), a spinach salad sprinkled with toasted pine nuts and drizzled with a creamy ranch dressing, and a basket of warm tortillas. To continue the Latin theme, finish by serving dulce de leche ice cream with sliced bananas and bittersweet chocolate sauce.

       2 tablespoons olive oil
    1¼ pounds ground beef, preferably chuck
       2 large onions, chopped
       2 tablespoons good quality chili powder
       1 tablespoon pumpkin pie spice
    One 28-ounce can diced tomatoes with green peppers
    One 14½-ounce can chicken broth
    ⅔ cup raisins
    ¼ cup cider vinegar
       Salt and freshly ground pepper

In a large, deep skillet, heat the oil over medium-high heat. Add the beef and the onions and cook, stirring to break up any large clumps of meat, until the beef begins to brown and the onions soften, 6 to 8 minutes. Add the chili powder and pumpkin pie spice and cook, stirring, for 1 minute.

Add the tomatoes, broth, raisins, and vinegar. Bring to a boil, reduce the heat to medium-low, and simmer, uncovered, for 15 minutes to blend the flavors. Adjust the consistency, if necessary, by adding more liquid or simmering a little longer to thicken to a spoonable stewlike consistency. Season to taste with salt and pepper. (The picadillo can be made up to 1 day ahead and refrigerated or frozen. Reheat gently.)

skillet
sweet and
sauerbraten *4 servings*

Making the classic German sauerbraten can involve
marinating the meat for several days and then cooking
it for several hours in a sweet and sour gravy. Our
shortened skillet version uses vinegar for the pleasantly
sour notes and for the sweet, crushed gingersnap
cookies, which also help to thicken the sauce. It's
delectable wintertime fare, especially when served with
braised sweet-and-sour red cabbage, buttered egg
noodles tossed with poppy seeds, and cherry strudel for
dessert.

$\frac{1}{4}$ cup light olive oil
$1\frac{1}{4}$ pounds thinly sliced round steaks
 Salt and freshly ground pepper
1 large onion, thinly sliced
1 bay leaf, broken in half
$\frac{1}{4}$ cup crushed gingersnap cookies
$\frac{1}{2}$ teaspoon ground allspice
One $14\frac{1}{2}$-ounce can beef broth
3 tablespoons red wine vinegar

In a large skillet, heat the oil. Season the steaks with
salt and pepper. When the oil is hot, sear the steaks
over medium-high to high heat until brown, about
1 minute per side. Transfer to a plate, leaving the
drippings in the pan. Reduce the heat to medium.

Add the onion and bay leaf to the pan drippings
and cook, stirring frequently, until the onions soften
and begin to brown, about 8 minutes. Add the
crushed cookies and the allspice and cook, stirring, for
1 minute. Whisk in the broth and cook, whisking frequently, until the sauce is smooth and thick, about
2 minutes. Stir in the vinegar.

Return the meat and any accumulated juices to
the sauce and simmer just to heat the meat through.
Season to taste with salt and pepper. (The sauerbraten
can be made up to 2 hours ahead and held at cool
room temperature, or refrigerated. Reheat gently.)

quick
corned beef
hash *4 servings*

You can use leftover corned beef for this hash, or buy a half-inch-thick slice of corned beef (one of the best of the deli meats, in our opinion) that you can then cut into nice, small cubes. And using frozen hash-brown potatoes, another favorite short-cut ingredient, really reduces prep time. The hash is great alone or topped with a poached egg. Good accompaniments are chunky salsa (or ketchup), a winter greens salad, and apple pie with a wedge of cheddar cheese for dessert.

5 cups frozen cubed (Southern-style) hash-brown
   potatoes, thawed
3 cups diced corned beef (12 ounces)
1 large green bell pepper, finely chopped
1 medium onion, chopped
2 tablespoons chopped fresh thyme or 2 teaspoons
   dried
1 teaspoon pepper, preferably coarsely ground
¼ cup light olive oil

In a large bowl, combine the potatoes, corned beef, bell pepper, onion, thyme, and pepper. Toss to blend well.

In a large skillet with a lid, heat the oil. Add the potato-meat mixture and press with a metal spatula to flatten. Cover the pan and cook the hash over medium heat until the bottom begins to crisp and brown, about 5 minutes. Using the spatula, turn the browned bottom in sections. Continue to cook, uncovered, turning over the browned bottom sections twice more, until the hash is thoroughly flecked with browned bits and the bell pepper and onion are softened, about 10 minutes.

Divide among 4 plates and serve.

calves' liver
with raisins
and onions *4 servings*

We love this sweet-tart, faintly Sicilian-style treatment of calves' liver, and it's especially wonderful with rice pilaf and sautéed escarole or broccoli rabe as side dishes. If fresh apricots are in season, serve them with mascarpone cheese for dessert. If not, substitute whatever fruit looks best in the market.

¼ cup raisins
¼ cup light olive oil
1¼ pounds calves' liver (about 8 thin slices)
   Salt and freshly ground pepper
1 large onion, thinly sliced
¼ cup balsamic or red wine vinegar

Place the raisins in a bowl, cover with ½ cup of warm water, and set aside to plump for 10 minutes. Do not drain.

In a large skillet, heat the oil. Pat the liver dry on paper towels and season on both sides with salt and pepper. Cook the liver over medium-high heat until browned outside but pink within, about 1 minute per side. (This may need to be done in two batches.) Transfer to a plate, leaving the drippings in the pan.

Add the onion to the skillet and cook over medium heat until browned and softened, about 8 minutes. Add the vinegar and raisins with their soaking water to the skillet, raise the heat to high, and cook, scraping up any browned bits on the bottom of the pan, until the liquid is reduced by about half, 1 to 2 minutes. Return the liver and any accumulated juices to the pan and heat gently. Season to taste with salt and pepper.

veal + lamb

Delicate veal is ideally suited to top-of-the-stove skillet cookery. For proof, all we need to do is ask the French and Italians, who have been masters at preparing veal for a couple of centuries now. In fact, just about the only way to cook the thinly sliced cut of veal called a scallop or cutlet is to quickly sauté the tender little medallion in butter and/or olive oil and finish the dish with a few simple (but judiciously added) seasonings. Several recipes in this chapter showcase this classic technique, including Veal Scallop Sauté with Gremolata Glaze (page 91) and Veal Saltimbocca with Fresh Sage (page 94). Likewise, meaty veal chops, which are so lean that they can dry out under the intense heat of a broiler or grill, also take beautifully to a quick browning in a heavy skillet. Pan-Seared and Braised Veal Chops Provençal (page 88) is our delicious case in point.

Lamb, which is perhaps more often associated with broiling than with panfrying, is so naturally juicy and full of flavor that it is the perfect base for such skillet-braised dishes as a speeded-up Moroccan Lamb and Dried Fruit Tagine (page 95), and rosemary-perfumed Lamb Chops Braised with White Beans and Tomatoes (page 98). And don't overlook the pricey but worth-every-penny Lamb Medallions with Garlic, Capers, and Mint (page 93), which calls for tender rounds cut from a boned out rack of lamb.

recipes

pan-seared and braised veal chops provençal *4 servings*

Veal is such a lean meat that it can dry out under the intense heat of a broiler or grill, so pan cooking meaty chops is the ideal method. Here the veal chops are first browned (for flavor) and then simmered in a sauce (which adds moistness). And such a lovely sauce it is—redolent of the flavors of the Provençal hills. This is a special main course that deserves thoughtful accompaniments, such as fettuccine buttered and tossed with Asiago cheese, sautéed mixed green vegetables (for example, zucchini and asparagus), and perhaps chocolate *pots de crème* with whipped cream for dessert.

4 veal chops, 1 to 1½ inches thick
  Salt and freshly ground pepper
4 tablespoons chopped fresh thyme
3 tablespoons butter
2 tablespoons olive oil
1 green or yellow bell pepper, thinly sliced
3 garlic cloves, finely chopped
¾ cup dry white wine
One 14½-ounce can Italian-style diced tomatoes

Season the veal chops on both sides with salt and pepper and sprinkle with 2 tablespoons of thyme, pressing it into the surface of the meat. In a large skillet, heat the butter and oil. Sauté the chops over medium-high heat until nicely browned on both sides, about 6 minutes total. Transfer to a plate, leaving the drippings in the pan.

Reduce the heat to medium. Add the bell pepper and garlic and cook, stirring frequently, until the pepper begins to wilt, about 3 minutes. Add the wine, bring to a boil, and cook for 1 minute, stirring up any browned bits that cling to the bottom of the pan. Add the tomatoes, return the veal and any accumulated juices to the skillet, and spoon some of the vegetables over the meat. Cook, uncovered, over medium heat until the meat is still juicy, but no longer pink inside, and the sauce is slightly reduced, about 10 minutes. Stir the remaining 2 tablespoons of thyme into the sauce and simmer for a couple of minutes to blend the flavors. (The dish can be made up to 1 hour ahead and set aside at cool room temperature. Reheat gently.)

Season to taste with salt and pepper before serving.

veal with artichokes and olives *4 servings*

Artichoke hearts packed in a jar are one of our favorite quick-cook ingredients—with the added plus that some of the piquant marinade can be used in a pan sauce to boost flavor. The flavors of the eastern Mediterranean predominate in this saucy veal dish, so continue the theme by prefacing the meal with a plate of stuffed grape leaves, and accompany the veal with orzo pilaf and steamed baby carrots tossed with mint. A dessert of purchased cheesecake sprinkled with chopped pistachio nuts would be perfection.

1¼	pounds veal scallops
	Salt and freshly ground pepper
¼	cup all-purpose flour
3	tablespoons fruity olive oil
Two	4-ounce jars marinated artichoke hearts, drained, with 3 tablespoons marinade reserved
1	cup chicken broth, preferably reduced-salt
¼ to ½	teaspoon crushed red pepper flakes
½	cup pitted and halved imported black olives
3	tablespoons chopped fresh oregano, plus sprigs for garnish

With a heavy skillet, meat mallet, or rolling pin, pound the veal to an even thickness of about ⅛ inch, then cut the veal into 3- to 4-inch pieces. Season the meat on both sides with salt and pepper. Put the flour on a plate and dredge the meat in the flour, shaking off the excess.

In a large skillet, heat the oil. Add the meat and cook over medium-high heat until nicely browned on both sides, about 5 minutes total. Transfer to a plate, leaving the drippings in the pan.

Add the drained artichokes and the 3 tablespoons of artichoke marinade to the pan drippings. Add the broth and pepper flakes, bring to a boil, and cook, stirring up any browned bits in the bottom of the pan, until slightly reduced, about 2 minutes. Return the meat and any accumulated juices to the pan, add the olives and oregano, and simmer over medium heat for 2 to 3 minutes to blend the flavors. (The dish can be made up to 1 hour ahead and set aside at cool room temperature or refrigerated. Reheat gently.)

Garnish with oregano sprigs before serving.

veal scallop sauté with gremolata glaze *4 servings*

Gremolata is the Italian word for a chopped parsley, garlic, and lemon zest mixture. It is most commonly used as a sprightly garnish sprinkled over osso buco, that long-simmered veal shank dish from Italy. However, we see no reason why such a good thing shouldn't be used with a lot more abandon, as we do here in this simple and quick-as-all-get-out veal sauté, where the gremolata becomes part of the pan sauce as well as the finishing garnish. Oven-roasted potatoes and other root vegetables would be a wonderful accompaniment to the veal, along with an arugula and radicchio salad. Finish with fresh figs or pears served with creamy mascarpone cheese.

- 2 lemons
- ⅓ cup chopped flat-leaf parsley
- 1 tablespoon chopped garlic
- 1¼ pounds veal scallops
- 4 tablespoons butter
  Salt and freshly ground pepper
- ¾ cup dry white wine

Grate 1 tablespoon of zest from the lemons and squeeze 2 tablespoons of juice. Set aside. In a small bowl, combine the lemon zest with the parsley and garlic to make the gremolata mixture.

With a heavy skillet, meat mallet, or rolling pin, pound the veal to an even thickness of about ⅛ inch, then cut the veal into 3- to 4-inch pieces. In a large skillet, heat 3 tablespoons of the butter. Season the meat on both sides with salt and pepper. Sauté the veal over medium-high heat until browned on both sides and cooked within, about 4 minutes total. Transfer to a plate, leaving the drippings in the pan.

Add the remaining tablespoon of butter to the skillet. Add half the parsley mixture and cook, stirring, for 1 minute. Add the wine, bring to a boil, and cook, stirring up any browned bits in the bottom of the pan, until reduced by about half, about 2 minutes. Add the lemon juice to the sauce.

Return the meat and any accumulated juices to the pan and simmer for about 2 minutes to heat through. Sprinkle with the remaining gremolata before serving.

lamb medallions with garlic, capers, and mint *4 servings*

One of the most elegant lamb dishes we know, this succulent sauté of buttery, tender medallions cut from the boneless lamb rack (also sometimes called the loin) is luxurious, special-occasion fare for sure. Don't be horrified at the cost. All lamb is expensive these days, but the best cuts are well worth it in terms of flavor and tenderness. We like oven-roasted baby potatoes and other vegetables with this, preceded or followed by a special salad of field greens sprinkled with chèvre and toasted walnuts. Finish with crème brûlée topped with fresh fruit.

1¼ pounds boneless rack of lamb, cut crosswise into ½-inch rounds
    Salt and freshly ground pepper
¼ cup chopped fresh mint, plus sprigs for garnish
2 tablespoons olive oil
2 garlic cloves, minced
1 plum tomato, seeded and diced
1 cup dry red wine
2 tablespoons butter, cut into about 8 pieces
2 tablespoons drained capers

Use the palm of your hand to flatten the lamb into ¼-inch-thick medallions. Season on both sides with salt and pepper and sprinkle with half the chopped mint, rubbing it into the meat.

In a large skillet, heat the oil. Add the lamb and cook over medium-high heat until well browned on both sides but still pink within, 1 to 2 minutes per side. Remove to a plate, leaving the drippings in the pan.

Add the garlic and diced tomato to the pan drippings and cook, stirring, for 1 minute. Add the wine, and bring to a boil, stirring up any browned bits on the bottom of the pan. Cook over medium-high heat until reduced by about half, 2 to 3 minutes. Remove from the heat, stir in the remaining half of the chopped mint, and add the butter, whisking until it melts into the sauce. Stir in the capers.

Spoon the sauce over the lamb, garnish with mint sprigs, and serve.

veal saltimbocca with fresh sage *4 servings*

Saltimbocca means "jump in the mouth," which is exactly what you want to say to these delectable little layerings of veal, prosciutto, and fontina cheese. Since saltimbocca is worthy of company fare, you'll want to make the rest of the meal equally special. Potatoes scalloped with herbs and cream, asparagus or *haricots verts* (thin French green beans), a light lettuce salad, and wedges of chocolate mousse cake sprinkled with raspberries would be fittingly festive accompaniments.

1¼ pounds veal scallops
   Salt and freshly ground pepper
1 tablespoon chopped fresh sage, plus sprigs
      for garnish
4 tablespoons butter
4 large, thin prosciutto slices (about 2 ounces total),
      halved
8 thin slices Italian fontina cheese (about 3 ounces)
2 tablespoons finely chopped shallots
½ cup Marsala

With a heavy skillet, meat mallet, or rolling pin, pound the veal to an even thickness of about ⅛ inch, then cut the veal into 8 pieces. Season the veal lightly with salt and generously with pepper. Sprinkle with the chopped sage, pressing it into the surface of the meat. In one very large skillet with a lid, or two medium skillets, heat the butter. Cook the veal slices over medium-high heat until brown on one side, 1 to 2 minutes. Turn over the meat. Layer 1 prosciutto slice and 1 cheese slice on the cooked side of each piece of veal. Cover the pan(s), reduce the heat to medium-low, and cook until the cheese melts, 1 to 2 minutes. Transfer to a platter, leaving the drippings in the pan, and tent with foil or keep warm in a slow oven while making the sauce.

Add the shallots to the pan drippings and cook, stirring, for 1 minute. Add the Marsala, raise the heat to high, and bring to a boil, stirring up any browned bits on the bottom of the pan.

Pour the sauce over the veal, garnish with the sage sprigs, and serve.

moroccan lamb
and dried fruit
tagine *4 servings*

Here's our version of a tagine, that long-simmered
North African lamb and dried fruit stew. Admittedly,
our skillet recipe takes some liberties with the classic
tagine, but we think that it retains the spirit of the
dish—plus it happens to taste just fabulous! Two
short-cut ingredients are featured here: readily available pumpkin pie spice, usually a blend of ground
cinnamon, nutmeg, and allspice; and mixed dried
fruits, which are often sold combined in one vacuum-
sealed bag. Natural accompaniments are steamed
couscous tossed with butter and chopped fresh herbs,
along with a platter of mixed pickled or grilled
vegetables, drizzled with thinned plain yogurt or a
creamy salad dressing. Scoops of pistachio ice cream,
along with cups of espresso, are the perfect finale.

1¼ pounds boneless leg of lamb, cut into
    2-inch chunks
1 medium onion, finely chopped
3 garlic cloves, finely chopped
2 teaspoons pumpkin pie spice
1 teaspoon ground cumin
½ teaspoon salt
½ teaspoon pepper
3 tablespoons fruity olive oil
One 14½-ounce can beef broth
1 cup mixed dried fruits (4 ounces), such as
    prunes, apples, apricots, and pears,
    coarsely chopped
1 lemon
2 tablespoons chopped parsley

In a large bowl, combine the lamb, onion, garlic,
pumpkin pie spice, cumin, salt, and pepper. Mix well
to combine, rubbing the seasoning ingredients evenly
into the meat.

In a large skillet with a lid, heat the oil. Cook the
meat over medium heat, turning on all sides, until
nicely browned, about 8 minutes. Add the broth, raise
the heat to high, and bring to a boil, stirring up any
browned bits on the bottom of the pan. Add the dried
fruits, reduce the heat to medium-low, and simmer,
covered, for 10 minutes.

Meanwhile, remove four ½-inch-wide strips of
zest from the lemon. Squeeze 1 tablespoon of juice.

Uncover the pan, add the lemon zest, and simmer
until the sauce is slightly reduced and thickened, 5 to
10 minutes. (The tagine can be made to this point up
to 1 day ahead and refrigerated. Reheat gently before
serving.)

Stir the lemon juice into the tagine, season to
taste with salt and pepper, sprinkle with the parsley,
and serve.

swedish meatballs in dill cream *4 servings*

What could be nicer than these delicate little meatballs nestled in a creamy, dill-flecked sauce? The sauce definitely calls for a side dish of buttered egg noodles tossed with caraway or poppy seeds, and perhaps, since the meatballs have a northern European bent, some braised red cabbage as well. Dessert should be something flavored with sweet spices, such as Swedish spice cookies, along with mugs of hot cinnamon tea.

$1\frac{1}{4}$ pounds ground veal
$\frac{1}{2}$ cup fresh white bread crumbs
$\frac{1}{2}$ cup finely chopped onion
1 large egg
2 tablespoons minced fresh dill
$\frac{3}{4}$ teaspoon salt
$\frac{1}{2}$ teaspoon freshly ground pepper
2 tablespoons butter
1 cup chicken broth
$\frac{2}{3}$ cup heavy cream

In a large bowl, combine the veal, bread crumbs, onion, egg, half the dill, and the salt and pepper. Use your fingers to blend lightly but thoroughly, and shape into 16 to 20 meatballs, each about 1 inch in diameter.

In a large skillet, heat the butter. Add the meatballs and cook over medium heat, turning frequently, until lightly browned all over and no longer pink within, about 10 minutes.

Push the meatballs to one side of the pan and add the chicken broth. Raise the heat to high, and cook, stirring up any browned bits, until reduced by about half, 2 to 3 minutes. Push the meatballs back toward the center of the pan. Add the cream and remaining dill and continue to boil until the sauce is slightly reduced and thickened, another 2 minutes or so. Season to taste with pepper; salt will probably not be needed since the broth will provide saltiness. (This dish can be made up to 1 hour ahead and set aside at cool room temperature. Reheat gently before serving.)

lamb chops braised with white beans and tomatoes *4 servings*

In France, lamb and beans are often paired together. It's a succulent combination, with the intense flavor of the meat (and the garlic!) contrasting beautifully with the mellow white beans. Wine, tomatoes, and rosemary each play important supporting roles, resulting in a dish that wins applause every time. Just add crusty peasant bread, a salad of bitter winter greens such as escarole, and a glass of red wine for a wonderfully satisfying supper.

    8 small rib or loin lamb chops, about 1 inch thick
      Salt and freshly ground pepper
    2 tablespoons chopped fresh rosemary
    3 tablespoons fruity olive oil
    3 garlic cloves, finely chopped
    1 cup dry white wine
One 14½-ounce can diced tomatoes flavored with
      green peppers and onions
    3 cups drained canned cannellini or other
      white beans

Season the lamb with salt and pepper and sprinkle with half the rosemary, rubbing it into the surface of the meat.

In a large, deep skillet, heat the oil. Cook the lamb chops over medium-high heat until browned on both sides, about 5 minutes. Push the chops to the side of the pan, add the garlic, and cook, stirring, for 1 minute.

Add the wine, raise the heat to high, and bring to a boil, stirring up any browned bits in the pan. Cook for 1 minute, then add the tomatoes, beans, and remaining half of the rosemary. Bring to a boil, reduce the heat to medium, and simmer, uncovered, until the mixture reduces and thickens slightly and the flavors blend, 10 to 15 minutes. (The stew can be made up to 1 day ahead and refrigerated. Reheat gently.)

Season to taste with salt and pepper, and serve.

north african kefta lamb patties *4 servings*

Ground lamb patties sing with flavor when seasoned with the aromatic spices and herbs of Morocco. Cayenne provides spiciness, so use the smaller quantity if your heat tolerance is on the low side. Serve with a deli tabbouleh or rice salad and pass bowls of diced tomatoes, diced cucumbers, and plain yogurt to spoon over the meat. A platter of seasonal fruit such as apricots or grapes, surrounded by an assortment of Middle Eastern pastries or honey cookies, is a fitting finish.

$1\frac{1}{4}$ pounds ground lamb
$\frac{1}{4}$ cup finely chopped onion
$\frac{1}{4}$ cup chopped fresh mint
$\frac{1}{4}$ cup chopped parsley
 1 teaspoon ground cumin
$\frac{1}{2}$ teaspoon ground cinnamon
$\frac{1}{4}$ to $\frac{1}{2}$ teaspoon cayenne pepper
$\frac{3}{4}$ teaspoon salt
$\frac{3}{4}$ teaspoon pepper
 1 tablespoon olive oil
 4 large romaine lettuce leaves

In a large bowl, combine the lamb, onion, mint, parsley, cumin, cinnamon, cayenne, salt, and pepper. Mix gently but thoroughly to combine and shape into 4 oval patties about $\frac{1}{2}$ inch thick.

In a large skillet, heat the oil. Add the patties and cook, turning once, over medium to medium-high heat until nicely browned on the outside and cooked to the desired degree of doneness within, about 10 minutes for medium.

Serve each patty on a romaine leaf.

spring lamb
stew with
baby vegetables *4 servings*

We love to make this elegant lamb stew for a spring-time dinner party. Like all saucy dishes, it can be made ahead and reheated—a value-added feature, especially for entertaining. Good accompaniments are parslied, steamed red-skinned potatoes, fat asparagus, and a lovely light lettuce salad. Pass a basket of buttery dinner rolls, and for dessert, a strawberry tart is perfect.

1¼ pounds lean boneless leg of lamb, cut into
        1-inch pieces (see Note)
3 tablespoons all-purpose flour
4 tablespoons chopped fresh thyme or
        1½ tablespoons dried
1 teaspoon salt
1 teaspoon pepper
4 tablespoons butter
3 garlic cloves, finely chopped
One 14½-ounce can beef broth
¾ pound peeled baby carrots, halved if large
1 cup frozen tiny pearl onions
1½ cups frozen peas

In a mixing bowl, combine the meat, flour, half the thyme, the salt, and pepper. Toss to thoroughly coat the meat with the flour and seasonings.

In a large, deep skillet with a lid, heat the butter over medium-high heat. Add the lamb and cook, turning the meat with tongs, until browned on all sides, about 5 minutes. Add the garlic and cook, stirring, for 1 minute. Add the broth, carrots, onions, and remaining half of the thyme. Bring to a boil, stirring up any browned bits on the bottom of the pan. Reduce the heat to medium-low, and cook, covered, until the carrots are tender, about 20 minutes. (The stew can be made to this point up to 1 day ahead and refrigerated. Reheat gently before proceeding.)

Add the peas and simmer for about 5 minutes until the peas are tender. Season to taste with salt and pepper before serving.

note:
Instead of using meat from the leg, you can buy loin lamb chops and remove the meat from the bone.

fish

We once knew a family who thought serving a fish dinner meant offering either frozen breaded fish sticks or tuna-noodle casserole. Well, times have really changed! Being New Englanders, we have always been able to choose from a huge array of fresh fish, and these days nearly every good supermarket anywhere in America has a seafood counter with fine quality fresh fish delivered at least several days a week. Now that we all know how good fish is for us, it has become the "new fast food" for home cooking.

Whether it is a delicate fillet of sole or a meaty tuna steak, all fish cooks rapidly, and indeed, the worst fate a fish can suffer in the pan is overcooking. The general rule of thumb is that fish should cook no more than 10 minutes per inch of thickness, making it the quickest main ingredient ever to jump in and out of a skillet.

In addition, fish are amazingly interchangeable—if the recipe calls for cod and you can only get catfish, that's fine. A knowledgeable fishmonger (that's the person behind the counter at a good fish market) will tell you what to substitute, so don't be put off from any of our recipes just because you can't get what we call for. For example, use swordfish in place of tuna for the Pan-Seared Tuna Paillards with Wasabi Pan Sauce (page 119), and use practically anything you like in Monkfish Cioppino (page 120) or Thai Fish Bouillabaisse (page 117). We make substitutions all the time, and trying a new variety is half the fun of eating fish. Fish is just plain wonderful; it's like having a company dinner any night of the week.

recipes

sole in browned butter and capers *4 servings*

Sole is a member of the flatfish family. There are many different types of sole, from gray to lemon to Dover. You can also use flounder, which can be more economical, or any other flat white fish in this classic French dish. Its preparation belies the notion that French cooking is long and involved, since it takes about ten minutes from start to finish. Chervil, with its delicate, lemony flavor, is lovely here, but flat-leaf parsley is just fine, too. In keeping with the rather elegant, springtime feel to this main course, we'd complete the plate with some steamed asparagus, roasted baby potatoes, and lemon tart for dessert.

- 1 cup milk
- ½ cup all-purpose flour
- 1¼ pounds sole, flounder, or other flat white fish fillets
- Salt and freshly ground pepper
- 4 tablespoons butter
- 1 tablespoon plus 1 teaspoon fresh lemon juice
- 2 tablespoons snipped fresh chives
- 1 tablespoon small capers
- 2 tablespoons chopped fresh chervil or parsley
- 4 lemon wedges

Pour the milk in a shallow dish and the flour in another shallow dish. Soak the fish in the milk for about 5 minutes, then dredge it in flour to coat both sides, shaking off the excess. Season the fish with salt and pepper.

In a large skillet, heat 2 tablespoons of the butter. Sauté the fish over medium-high heat, turning once, until golden brown on both sides and cooked through, about 5 minutes total. Transfer the fish to a platter.

Add the remaining 2 tablespoons of butter to the skillet and cook, stirring, over medium heat, until the butter is nutty brown and fragrant. Stir in the lemon juice, chives, capers, and half of the chervil.

Spoon the sauce over the fish, then sprinkle with the remaining chervil and garnish with the lemon wedges.

sole
francese *4 servings*

This is a dish served at almost every old-fashioned traditional Italian restaurant in Connecticut, where we
live. However, we have never found a recipe for it in
any Italian cookbook, which leaves us thinking that
this is a regional Italian-American preparation. To con-
fuse the issue even more, it means "French sole" in
Italian, but seems to turn up only on Italian menus.
Whatever the origin, it is really good, and so we came
up with our own home-style rendition. In the Italian
restaurants near us, it is served with a side of spaghetti
with marinara sauce, steamed zucchini, and lots of
Italian bread. Why tamper with success?

  2 lemons
  ½ cup all-purpose flour
  ½ teaspoon salt
  ¼ teaspoon pepper
  ½ cup milk
  2 large eggs
  1 pound sole fillets, cut into 8 pieces
  ¼ cup olive oil

Grate 2 teaspoons of zest from one of the lemons. Cut
the other lemon into 8 wedges.

   On a plate, stir together the flour, salt, and
pepper. In a small mixing bowl, whisk together the
milk, eggs, and grated lemon zest.

   Dip the fish into the milk mixture, then dredge
in the flour, then back into the milk mixture, and
again into the flour.

   In a large skillet, heat the oil. Cook the fish over
medium heat, taking care that the pieces do not touch
one another, until golden brown and crusty on one
side, about 4 minutes. Use a spatula to turn the fish,
taking care not to dislodge the golden crust. Cook
until the other side is golden brown and crusty, about
4 minutes.

   Transfer the fish to 4 serving plates and garnish
with the lemon wedges.

beer-battered
fried fish with malt vinegar
tartar sauce *4 servings*

Fish 'n' chips, a staple of London pubs, are deep-fried hunks of white fish served with French fries. The whole thing is often wrapped in newspaper and served with tartar sauce and malt vinegar. Taking great liberties here, we panfry the fish, which we think gives the very same result, pop frozen French fries in the oven, and combine the malt vinegar and tartar sauce ideas into one great warm dip. We won't tamper with the classic newspaper-wrapped presentation, since that already fits our timesaving theme—no dishes to wash!

1 cup all-purpose flour

1 teaspoon baking soda

½ teaspoon salt

½ teaspoon pepper

1 cup flat ale or beer

4 tablespoons malt vinegar

Vegetable oil for panfrying

1 pound cod, grouper, or other white fish, cut into 1½- to 2-inch chunks

⅓ cup mayonnaise

1 tablespoon chopped fresh tarragon

In a mixing bowl, whisk together the flour, baking soda, salt, pepper, ale, and 2 tablespoons of the vinegar until smooth.

In a large skillet, heat ¼ to ½ inch of oil until a crust of bread sizzles and turns gold when dropped into it.

While the oil is heating, dip the fish into the batter to coat completely. Fry the fish pieces so that they do not touch each other, in two batches if necessary, and turning once, until the batter is crisp and rich golden brown and the fish is cooked through, 6 to 8 minutes total. Using tongs, transfer the fish to paper towels to drain.

Pour off all but 1 tablespoon of oil from the skillet. Stir in the mayonnaise, tarragon, and remaining 2 tablespoons of vinegar. Stir until smooth and heated through, about 1 minute.

Serve the fish with the warm tartar sauce passed separately for dipping.

panfried catfish fingers on warm lemon slaw *4 servings*

Catfish can be fixed many ways, and entire cookbooks are devoted to this versatile fish. Our hands-down favorite way to cook it is to panfry it in a peppery and lemony cornmeal coating. Since much of America's catfish comes from farms in the Ozarks of Arkansas, this Deep-South treatment seems natural and right. Setting the fish on top of warm, lemony coleslaw is a down-home idea that went uptown, especially since packaged coleslaw mixtures now eliminate slicing all that cabbage. Some other easy sides are stewed okra and canned tomatoes seasoned with fresh thyme, frozen shoestring French fries, and a bakery-made peach pie.

1 large lemon
½ cup yellow cornmeal
½ teaspoon salt
½ teaspoon coarsely ground pepper
1 pound catfish fillets, cut into ¾-by-2-inch
    lengthwise strips
4 tablespoons vegetable oil
3 cups packaged coleslaw mix

Grate 1 teaspoon of zest from the lemon and squeeze 2 tablespoons of juice. Set aside.

In a shallow dish, stir together the cornmeal, salt, pepper, and grated lemon zest. Rinse the catfish lightly under cold water, then dredge in the cornmeal mixture to coat all sides.

In a large skillet, heat 2 tablespoons of the oil. Panfry the catfish over medium-high heat, turning once or twice, until the coating is golden brown and crisp, and the fish is cooked through, 5 to 7 minutes. Transfer the fish to a platter.

Add the remaining 2 tablespoons of oil and the lemon juice to the skillet. Add the coleslaw mix and toss over medium heat until the coleslaw is coated and just begins to soften, 1 to 2 minutes. Season to taste with salt and pepper.

Serve the fish placed on a bed of coleslaw.

poached turbot with pink aïoli *4 servings*

Turbot is a mild white fish, similar to and interchangeable with red snapper, rockfish, and grouper. It is a fish
largely caught in European waters, so this rather
European aïoli sauce is right at home with it. But if
you can't get turbot, feel free to substitute whatever is
freshest and most appealing in your market. Any combination of herbs that you have on hand or in the
garden will work here. We especially like tarragon,
parsley, and chives with fish, but dill, thyme, or basil
would also be delicious. It's nice to include parsley for
sharpness and chives for their mild onion taste, and
these are usually readily available. Braised tiny peas
and pearl onions, a crusty baguette, and a salad of
mixed European-style greens would complement the
turbot nicely.

1¼ pounds turbot fillets, cut into 4 equal pieces
     Salt and freshly ground pepper
¾   cup dry white wine or bottled clam juice, plus
     additional as needed
3   tablespoons tarragon white wine vinegar
¼   cup plus 2 tablespoons chopped mixed
     fresh herbs
3   tablespoons mayonnaise
1   tablespoon regular or herbed tomato paste

Season the fish with salt and pepper. Pour the wine,
vinegar, and 1 cup of water into a medium skillet.
Add ¼ cup of the herbs and the fish. The liquid
should barely cover the fish, if it does not, add a little
more wine. Bring to a simmer over medium heat,
then reduce the heat to medium-low and poach the
fish gently until it is cooked through, 6 to 8 minutes.
Transfer the fish to a platter.

Raise the heat to high and boil the poaching
liquid until it is reduced by about half, 2 to 4 minutes. Strain the liquid through a fine-mesh sieve into a
bowl. Return ⅓ cup of the liquid to the pan and dis-
card the rest. Bring to a simmer over medium-low
heat. Reduce the heat to low, whisk in the mayonnaise
and tomato paste, and continue whisking until the
sauce becomes frothy, about 1 minute. Whisk in the
remaining 2 tablespoons of herbs. Season to taste with
salt and pepper.

Spoon about 2 tablespoons of the reduced
poaching liquid into each of 4 rimmed plates or
shallow soup bowls. Add the turbot, then spoon the
sauce over the fish.

honey mustard–seared salmon and caramelized shallots with watercress *4 servings*

Salmon has become one of the most affordable fishes, largely because it is often farm raised. Because farmed fish don't get a lot of exercise, they tend to get a little plump, a concept we all understand pretty well if we don't go to the gym for a few weeks. The good news for salmon is that fat is fine, since it contains the omega oil that nutritionists tell us is the good kind of fat for our cholesterol. That said, the crème fraîche probably cancels the benefits of the omega oil, but it sure is good for the palate. Keep the side dishes light and colorful, such as steamed baby carrots, sautéed cherry tomatoes, and an herbed orzo pilaf.

1¼ pounds skinless salmon fillet, cut into
    4 equal pieces
    Salt and freshly ground pepper
2 tablespoons honey mustard
3 tablespoons butter
¼ cup chopped shallots
⅔ cup dry white wine
⅓ cup crème fraîche or heavy cream
1 cup watercress sprigs

Season the salmon lightly with salt and generously with pepper. Smear the fish on both sides with the mustard.

In a large skillet, heat 2 tablespoons of the butter. Sear the salmon over high heat, turning once, until browned on both sides and just cooked through, about 8 minutes. Use a spatula to transfer the salmon to a platter. Add the remaining 1 tablespoon of butter to the skillet and cook the shallots over medium-high heat, stirring until golden, 1 to 2 minutes. Reduce the heat to medium, add the wine, and simmer for 2 minutes. Reduce the heat to medium-low, stir in the crème fraîche, and simmer, stirring, until heated through. Season to taste with salt and pepper. Return the fish to the sauce just to heat through, about 30 seconds.

Arrange the salmon on a platter or on 4 plates. Spoon the sauce over the fish, then top with the watercress sprigs.

scandinavian double salmon and dill cakes *4 servings*

Some of the best ideas for salmon come from North Atlantic countries, which is no surprise since this cold-water fish is a staple in these cold-weather countries, where it is loved both fresh and smoked. These fish cakes are inspired by some of the classic ingredients of Scandinavian cuisine—dill, mustard, onion, and rye bread. Smoked salmon varies widely in price, and for this recipe you don't need to break the bank. Buy what you like and can afford. The dish is presented as an open-faced sandwich (another Scandinavian specialty), and all that is needed to complete the meal is a tossed salad with a creamy dressing, and a simple steamed vegetable medley such as peas and carrots.

- 6 slices rye bread, torn into small pieces
- 12 ounces skinless salmon fillet, cut into 1-inch chunks
- 2 ounces smoked salmon, cut into 1-inch pieces
- 2½ tablespoons Dijon mustard
- 2 tablespoons chopped fresh dill, plus sprigs for garnish
- ½ teaspoon pepper
- 2 tablespoons butter
- 4 thin slices red onion
- 4 thin slices tomato

In a food processor, whirl 2 slices of the bread to make about 1 cup of crumbs. Set aside.

In the same food processor bowl, pulse together the fresh salmon and smoked salmon until finely chopped. Add 1½ tablespoons of the mustard, the dill, pepper, and ⅔ cup of the reserved bread crumbs and process until well blended, about 20 seconds. Use your hands to form 8 small cakes from the salmon mixture. Place the remaining ⅓ cup of bread crumbs on a plate and dip the salmon cakes into the crumbs to lightly coat.

In a large skillet, heat the butter. Cook the salmon cakes over medium heat, turning once with a spatula, until browned on both sides and cooked through, 6 to 8 minutes total. (The salmon cakes can be prepared up to 30 minutes ahead and kept warm in a 200-degree oven.)

Lightly toast the remaining 4 slices of rye bread, then spread with the remaining 1 tablespoon of mustard. Arrange 2 salmon cakes, slightly overlapping, on each slice of toast, then top with the onion and tomato slices. Garnish with the dill sprigs.

trout
amandine *4 servings*

This is the simplest, and some think the best, method for cooking fresh trout. If you catch them yourself, you will probably want to show off and cook them whole, but we, who do most of our fishing in the market, are perfectly content to make it really easy and cook trout fillets. Other flatfish fillets, such as sole or flounder, can be prepared in this same manner. Since trout season is a harbinger of spring in our New England region, we always think of roasted new potatoes and steamed asparagus as the natural accompaniments. Strawberry shortcake is always the perfect springtime dessert.

3 tablespoons all-purpose flour
$\frac{1}{2}$ teaspoon salt
$\frac{1}{4}$ teaspoon freshly ground pepper
4 trout fillets (1 to $1\frac{1}{4}$ pounds total)
4 tablespoons butter
$\frac{1}{2}$ cup sliced almonds
$1\frac{1}{2}$ tablespoons fresh lemon juice
2 tablespoons chopped parsley
2 tablespoons snipped fresh chives

On a plate, stir together the flour, salt, and pepper. Dredge the trout in the seasoned flour to lightly coat.

In a large skillet, heat $2\frac{1}{2}$ tablespoons of the butter and sauté the trout over medium-high heat, turning once with a spatula, until golden brown and cooked through, 4 to 6 minutes total. Use a spatula to transfer the fish to a plate.

Add the remaining $1\frac{1}{2}$ tablespoons of butter to the skillet. Toss the almonds over medium heat until rich golden brown and fragrant, about 2 minutes. Stir in the lemon juice and 1 tablespoon each of the parsley and chives.

To serve, spoon the sauce over the fish and sprinkle with the remaining tablespoon each of parsley and chives.

red snapper
with warm
mango salsa *4 servings*

Red snapper is a particularly pretty fish fillet, but grouper or catfish are good substitutes in this recipe if you can't find snapper. Warming the mango salsa in the skillet brings out the sweetness of the fruit, the heat of the jalapeño, the sourness of the lime, and the light, briny flavor of the saltwater fish. It pleases all the taste buds and is a feast for the eyes, too. Roasted sweet potato slices and a salad of light greens with a creamy dressing are good accompaniments.

  1 large lime
  3 tablespoons light olive oil
1¼ pounds red snapper fillets, cut into 4 equal pieces
    Salt and freshly ground pepper
  1 mango, peeled and diced (about 2 cups)
 ½ cup coarsely chopped red onion
  1 small jalapeño, seeded and finely chopped
  2 tablespoons chopped cilantro

Grate 1 teaspoon of zest from the lime and squeeze 2 tablespoons of juice. Set them aside.

In a large skillet, heat the oil. Season the fish lightly with salt and pepper, then cook over medium heat, turning once, until the fish is cooked through, 6 to 8 minutes total. Transfer the fish to a plate.

Add the lime juice and zest to the skillet, scraping up any browned bits clinging to the bottom of the pan. Add the mango, onion, jalapeño, and cilantro. Reduce the heat to medium-low and cook, stirring, until everything is heated through and the mango just begins to soften, about 2 minutes. Season to taste with salt and pepper.

Serve the fish with the salsa ladled on top.

thai
fish
bouillabaisse *4 servings*

No, this is not a bouillabaisse; we just like the word. Indeed, coastal cuisines around the world, from the Mediterranean to Asia, have aromatic fish stews in their repertoires. Here the secret ingredient is fish sauce. If you have not used it before, trust us, don't take a whiff of the bottle. Just add it to the recipe. In the bottle, it smells like a cross between old fish and old socks. In the recipe, it is ambrosial. We know it's a leap of culinary faith, but all of Thailand has gone before you, and everyone there is just fine. If you have a worry, it should be about the curry paste, since it is super-hot and spicy, requiring the tempering of the sweet coconut milk. About the coconut milk, be sure it is the Asian unsweetened variety and not the sweet coconut cream of piña colada fame. Packaged broccoli slaw is found next to the coleslaw mix in the produce section. It looks and tastes terrific here. This soup is even better with a spoonful of aromatic jasmine rice, either alongside or plopped right into the soup bowl. Accompany with a light salad and finish with sliced tropical fruit and ginger cookies.

2 limes
$2\frac{1}{2}$ cups unsweetened coconut milk
2 tablespoons Thai red curry paste
2 tablespoons Thai fish sauce
$1\frac{1}{4}$ pounds red snapper, turbot, or sea bass fillets, cut into 1½-inch chunks
2 cups packaged broccoli slaw mix
⅓ cup chopped cilantro

From $1\frac{1}{2}$ of the limes, grate 2 teaspoons of zest and squeeze 2 tablespoons juice. Thinly slice the remaining ½ lime. Set it all aside.

In a large, deep skillet over low heat, whisk together the coconut milk and curry paste until smooth. Whisk in 1 cup of water, the fish sauce, and the reserved lime zest and juice. Bring to a simmer over medium heat. (The bouillabaisse base can be prepared to this point up to 4 hours ahead and refrigerated. Reheat gently.) Add the fish and return the liquid to a simmer. Reduce the heat to medium-low and simmer gently until the fish is nearly cooked through, about 5 minutes. Add the broccoli slaw mix and simmer until the vegetables are barely tender and the fish is cooked through, about 3 minutes more. Stir in half of the cilantro.

Serve the fish in shallow soup bowls sprinkled with the remaining cilantro and with a lime slice floating in the center of each one.

cod braised with potatoes and golden onions

4 servings

This is a skillet relative to New England clam chowder, probably our favorite fish soup. When done well, clam chowder is simple and has few ingredients except fish, onion, potato, broth, and maybe a little thyme. Taking a cue from this simple Yankee wisdom, not much more is added here. Serve with a bowl of chowder biscuits (thick, crisp crackers) or hard rolls and a big spinach salad tossed with crumbled bacon. For dessert, find a bakery that makes Boston cream pie (which is really a cake, but that's another cookbook).

    2 tablespoons butter
    1 medium onion, thinly sliced
    ¾ pound small red potatoes, cut into ½-inch dice
    3 tablespoons chopped fresh thyme, plus sprigs
        for garnish
    ½ cup heavy cream
    ½ cup dry white wine
    ½ cup bottled clam juice
    1¼ pounds cod fillets, cut into 1-inch strips or chunks
      Salt and freshly ground pepper

In a large, deep skillet with a lid, heat the butter. Cook the onion and potatoes over medium heat, stirring often, until the potatoes are nearly cooked through and the onion is tinged with gold, about 6 minutes. Stir in 2 tablespoons of the chopped thyme, the cream, wine, and clam juice. (The recipe can be prepared up to 30 minutes ahead to this point and kept at cool room temperature.) Bring to a simmer, and add the fish. Reduce the heat to medium-low, cover the pan, and simmer, stirring gently once or twice, until the fish is cooked through and the potatoes are tender. Stir in the remaining 1 tablespoon of chopped thyme and season to taste with salt and pepper.

Serve in shallow soup bowls, garnished with thyme sprigs.

pan-seared tuna paillards with wasabi pan sauce *4 servings*

In this recipe, the tuna is cut thinner than usual, so that there will be more "crust." It is important to cook it over high heat so that it sears quickly on both sides while leaving the interior barely pink. Serve the tuna with ginger-spiked scalloped potatoes and stir-fried snow peas. Since this is a rather elegant dish, be sure to plan for an equally lovely dessert, such as coconut rice pudding topped with sliced pineapple and mango.

¼ cup sesame seeds
1¼ pounds tuna steaks, cut about ½ inch thick
2 teaspoons sesame oil
3 tablespoons peanut oil
1½ teaspoons wasabi powder
½ cup dry white wine
1 tablespoon soy sauce

Place the sesame seeds on a plate. Lightly brush the tuna with the sesame oil, then dip into the sesame seeds, patting them on with your hands. The seeds may not completely coat the fish.

In a large skillet, heat the peanut oil. Cook the tuna over high heat until seared on both sides and the seeds are browned, carefully turning once, about 4 minutes total. Some of the seeds will fall off when the fish is turned; they will become part of the sauce.

Transfer the tuna to a plate. Reduce the heat to medium. Stir the wasabi powder into the pan drippings, then stir in the wine and soy sauce. Simmer over medium heat, stirring, until the wasabi powder is dissolved and the thin sauce is smooth, about 2 minutes.

Serve the tuna with the sauce dribbled over it.

monkfish
cioppino *4 servings*

Cioppino is the San Francisco version of bouillabaisse. Actually, fish stews are a part of nearly every seacoast country's cuisine, but we especially like the earthy broth flavored with fennel, tomato, garlic, and red wine that is typical of both bouillabaisse and cioppino. Fish stew is usually made with whatever is the catch of the day, and you can feel free to substitute nearly any fish, shellfish, or combination for the monkfish. Some people say monkfish tastes like lobster, so use that if you are feeling flush. Be sure to offer a basket of sourdough bread to sop up all that savory broth, and accompany the cioppino with a salad of mixed California-style greens in a wine vinaigrette. San Francisco is noted for its chocolate, and chocolate in any form is appropriate for dessert anytime.

¼ cup extra-virgin olive oil
1½ cups coarsely chopped fennel (about 6 ounces)
1 medium green bell pepper, coarsely chopped
1 medium onion, coarsely chopped
4 large garlic cloves, finely chopped
Two 14½-ounce cans Italian-style diced tomatoes
1 cup bottled clam juice
1 cup dry red or white wine
1¼ pounds monkfish or other firm fish fillets,
    cut into 1½-inch chunks
Salt and freshly ground pepper

In a large, deep skillet, heat the olive oil. Cook the fennel, bell pepper, and onion over medium heat, stirring often, until softened, about 4 minutes. Add the garlic and cook for 30 seconds. Add the tomatoes, clam juice, and wine. Bring to a simmer. (The cioppino base can be prepared to this point up to 4 hours ahead and refrigerated. Reheat gently.) Add the fish, and simmer over medium-low heat until it is cooked through, 7 to 10 minutes. Season to taste with salt and pepper.

Serve the fish and broth in shallow soup bowls.

shellfish

We are often asked how much shrimp to buy for a party. The answer is always that it doesn't matter. People will eat as much shrimp as you offer. There are never any left over. That's because shrimp, and most of its shellfish relatives, have universal appeal. Even people who say they don't like fish order crab cakes in restaurants, and shrimp scampi is a perennial favorite on menus. People like to cook shellfish at home, too. Somehow, shrimp just seem approachable—no bones, and they even come peeled and deveined (a little more pricey, but a whole lot quicker). Scallops are just as quick and simple. Most of today's mussels are farm raised in a pristine environment, so instead of scrubbing off barnacles and sand, you need only give them a mere shower under running water. Thanks to better shipping, several varieties of utterly fresh clams are available in even the most land-locked areas.

The versatility of shellfish is nearly endless, which is why we had the hardest time whittling this chapter down—we could have done a whole *Flash in the Pan* on shellfish! Maybe it's because shellfish are native to local waters from Asia to the Mediterranean, and every region of the United States as well. This chapter is probably more global than any other, with stream-lined classic recipes such as Quick Curried Shrimp (page 128) and Mussels Oreganata with Leeks and Cream (page 137). In America, we love Peel 'n' Eat Key Lime BBQ Shrimp (page 124) from the warm waters of the Gulf of Mexico, Crab Cakes and Mustard Tartar Sauce (page 134) from the Chesapeake Bay, Herbed Clam Hash (page 133) from New England waters, Oysters Rockefeller Stew (page 139) from New Orleans, and Shrimp Pilau (page 131) from the low country of the Carolinas.

All seafood is quick cooking, which is why it fits in so well with today's culinary lifestyles. In response to hugely increased demand, good supermarkets everywhere now stock excellent fish and shellfish. That's good news for us, and you!

recipes

peel 'n' eat
key lime
bbq shrimp *4 servings*

Key limes, which have their own distinctive flavor, are
hard to find outside of Florida, so feel free to substitute
regular limes, which incidentally are called Persian
limes. Start out with the lesser amount of hot-pepper
sauce, then add more as needed—every brand has its
own degree of heat. The subtropical flavors accentuated
here would be enhanced by a basket of crusty Cuban
bread and a rice salad spiked with chopped cilantro
and green onions. Don't forget lots of napkins.

- 4 Key limes or 2 Persian limes
- 4 tablespoons butter
- 4 large garlic cloves, finely chopped
- 1½ tablespoons Worcestershire sauce
- 1 pound extra-large shrimp in the shell
- ¼ to ½ teaspoon hot-pepper sauce, to taste
- ¼ cup chopped parsley

Cut 4 thin slices from one of the limes, then grate
1 teaspoon of zest and squeeze 2 tablespoons of juice
from the rest of the limes.

In a large skillet, heat the butter, garlic,
Worcestershire sauce, and lime zest and juice until
bubbly. Add the shrimp. Cook over medium heat,
stirring often, until the shrimp just begin to turn
pink and are nearly cooked through, about 3 minutes.
Stir in the hot sauce and cook 1 minute more. Stir in
the parsley. Taste and add additional hot sauce, if
desired.

Serve the shrimp with the sauce, garnish with the
lime slices, and let everyone peel and eat them with
their fingers.

shrimp in
basil lemongrass
broth *4 servings*

Lemongrass and Thai basil are herbs used often in Thai cooking, but until recently they were nearly impossible to find in mainstream American markets. Today, both are much more common. If you can't find fresh lemongrass, however, try reconstituting the dried version that is now available in the spice section of the store. Or, substitute 1 teaspoon of grated lemon zest for 1 tablespoon of lemongrass (the flavor will be more lemony and less flowery). If you can't find fresh Thai basil, just use a mix of ordinary Mediterranean basil and some fresh mint, which together will nearly approximate the taste of Thai basil. Accompany this sophisticated supper with steamed rice, and a salad of light greens sprinkled with unsprayed edible flower petals, such as nasturtiums, if you have them. Finish with a plate of sliced Pacific fruits, such as pineapple, kiwi, and star fruit.

1 cup canned unsweetened coconut milk
¾ cup dry white wine
1½ tablespoons Thai fish sauce
2 cups thinly sliced mix of red, green, and yellow bell peppers
1 tablespoon finely chopped fresh ginger
2 tablespoons finely chopped fresh lemongrass (tender parts only)
1¼ pounds medium shrimp, peeled and deveined
3 tablespoons chopped fresh Thai basil
Salt and freshly ground pepper
1 lime, cut into wedges

In a medium skillet, bring the coconut milk, wine, and fish sauce to a simmer over medium heat. Add the bell peppers, ginger, and lemongrass. Reduce the heat to medium-low and simmer until the peppers are crisp-tender, about 3 minutes. Add the shrimp and basil. Simmer until the shrimp turn pink, 2 to 3 minutes. Season to taste with salt and pepper.

Serve the shrimp and broth in shallow soup bowls, garnished with lime wedges for squeezing into the broth.

stir-fried
five-spice shrimp
and snow peas *4 servings*

Chinese five-spice powder is a great ingredient to have on hand. It's a mixture of anise, ginger, licorice root, cinnamon, and cloves, and gives a wonderfully complex flavor to the simplest of stir-fries, such as this one, which uses only seven ingredients and takes about five minutes to prepare. To turn your house into a Chinese restaurant, start the meal with some purchased egg rolls, then accompany the stir-fry with steamed rice. For dessert, buy some fortune cookies and serve with pineapple chunks—it will be like homemade take-out.

1¼ pounds large shrimp, peeled and deveined
2 teaspoons Chinese five-spice powder
3 tablespoons peanut or vegetable oil
½ pound snow peas, halved if large
1 tablespoon rice wine vinegar
1 tablespoon soy sauce
¼ cup thinly sliced green onions

Sprinkle the shrimp with the five-spice powder. In a large skillet, heat the oil. Stir-fry the shrimp over medium-high heat just until they turn pink, 2 to 3 minutes. Add the snow peas and stir-fry until crisp-tender, about 1 minute. Add the vinegar, soy sauce, and green onions. Simmer for 30 seconds, and serve.

quick
curried
shrimp *4 servings*

Depending upon your personal experience, curry can
be positively heavenly, or absolutely hellish. The
secrets to a tasty curry are using a good quality, fresh
curry powder, and using it with restraint. Like many
ground spice mixtures, curry powder loses its potency
quickly, after about six months, so unless you cook a
lot of curry, buy the best quality you can find in a
small quantity and replace it often. Add curry to your
dishes during the cooking process, not at the end,
when it will still have a raw, unpleasant taste. Curry is
versatile, and is especially well suited to shellfish, particularly shrimp. This very simple version is best
served with plain rice and sautéed baby carrots and
sugar snap peas. If your curry powder is hot or you are
liberal with the cayenne, you will especially appreciate
a scoop of vanilla ice cream for dessert.

1¼ pounds extra-large or large shrimp, peeled
    and deveined
1½ tablespoons curry powder
⅛ teaspoon cayenne or more to taste
2 tablespoons vegetable oil
1 medium onion, chopped
One 14½-ounce can diced tomatoes with green
    pepper and onion
1 tablespoon fresh lemon juice
¼ cup chopped cilantro
  Salt and freshly ground pepper

Sprinkle the shrimp with the curry powder and
cayenne.

In a large skillet, heat the oil and cook the onion
over medium heat, stirring often, until just softened,
about 4 minutes. Add the shrimp and cook, stirring,
until they just begin to turn pink, about 2 minutes.
Add the tomatoes and lemon juice. Simmer, stirring
often, until the shrimp turn completely pink and are
cooked through, about 3 minutes. Stir in the cilantro
and cook for 30 seconds. Season to taste with salt and
pepper.

tarragon shrimp scampi *4 servings*

Shrimp scampi is an all-American favorite in Italian restaurants. Scampi are not shrimp, but they are related, and because the real thing is rarely available here, we've come to expect scampi to be shrimp. If that sounds confusing, never mind, since anything simmered in butter, olive oil, wine, and herbs will taste good. Here, scampi are really pretty served alongside nests of swirled cooked cappellini. Of course, lots of Italian bread will serve the same tasty purpose—to sop up the extra sauce. Sliced zucchini braised in a little broth, then dotted with roasted red peppers makes a simple, succulent vegetable side dish. The most popular all-American dessert served in Italian restaurants is ricotta cheesecake, so we say go to an Italian bakery and buy one.

- 2 tablespoons butter
- 2 tablespoons olive oil
- 6 large garlic cloves, thinly sliced
- 1¼ pounds large shrimp, peeled and deveined
- ⅔ cup dry white wine
- 2 tablespoons chopped fresh tarragon
  Salt and freshly ground pepper

In a large skillet, heat the butter and oil. Cook the garlic and shrimp over medium heat, stirring often, until the shrimp begin to turn pink, about 2 minutes. Add the wine and half of the tarragon. Simmer until the shrimp are pink, 2 to 3 minutes. Stir in the remaining half of the tarragon and season to taste with salt and pepper.

prosciutto-wrapped
sambuca shrimp *4 servings*

You can eat these with forks or your fingers. Served on
a platter, they make a wonderful hors d'oeuvre, but
since your guests will want more, you might as well
serve them for supper. If you want to make a real show,
do this tableside over a portable burner, adding the
liqueur at the end and igniting it for a spectacular
flambéed sauce to pour over the shrimp. Even if you
don't go for pyrotechnics, orzo sprinkled with green
onions and red pepper look pretty with the shrimp, as
do steamed asparagus spears. For dessert, we'd favor
fresh figs split and stuffed with a little sweetened mascarpone cheese and drizzled with a little more
sambuca.

   3 ounces very thinly sliced prosciutto
 1¼ pounds extra-large shrimp, peeled and deveined
   3 tablespoons olive oil
   ½ cup orange juice
   2 tablespoons fresh lemon juice
   2 tablespoons sambuca or other anise liqueur

Cut the prosciutto into long, 1- to 1½-inch-wide
strips. Wrap the strips around the shrimp. They
should stick to the shrimp without toothpicks.

In a large skillet, heat the oil. Cook the
prosciutto-wrapped shrimp over medium-high heat,
turning once or twice, until the prosciutto is crisped
and the shrimp turn pink and are cooked through,
4 to 5 minutes. Transfer the shrimp to a heat-proof
plate.

Add the orange and lemon juices to the skillet,
stirring until the mixture comes to a boil. If you plan
to flambé the shrimp, pour the liqueur over the juices,
remove the pan from the heat, and ignite with a long
match. If you are not going to flambé the shrimp,
simply stir in the liqueur and simmer for about 1
minute.

Pour the sauce over the shrimp and serve.

shrimp pilau *4 servings*

In the low country of the Carolinas, pilau is a favorite
dish. A close cousin to the jambalayas of New Orleans,
this is home style, peasant cooking based on local
ingredients and flavors. Some say pilau means "pilaf,"
but who knows? It is an easy, downright tasty one-dish
supper, that's for sure. Serve it with a big salad of baby
dandelion greens with a warm bacon dressing and a
basket of corn sticks. Finish with another Southern
classic, coconut layer cake.

 3 tablespoons olive oil
 1 medium onion, chopped
 1 medium green bell pepper, chopped
 3 large garlic cloves, finely chopped
 1 cup long-grain white rice
 2 cups bottled clam juice
One 14½-ounce can diced Italian-style tomatoes
 1¼ pounds medium or large shrimp, peeled and
   deveined
  Salt and freshly ground pepper

In a large skillet with a lid, heat the oil. Cook the
onion and bell pepper over medium heat, stirring
often, until just softened, about 4 minutes. Add the
garlic and cook, stirring, for 1 minute. Add the rice
and stir until coated with oil. Add the clam juice and
bring to a simmer. Cover the skillet, reduce the heat
to medium-low, and simmer for 15 minutes.

 Uncover, stir in the tomatoes, then add the
shrimp, pushing them down into the rice. Cover the
skillet again and simmer until the liquid is absorbed
and the shrimp turn pink and are cooked through,
about 5 minutes. Season to taste with salt and generous amounts of pepper. (The pilau can be kept warm
for about 30 minutes. If it begins to dry out, stir in a
little water or clam juice.)

shrimp español *4 servings*

We'd use jumbo shrimp to make a really spectacular presentation here, but large or extra-large shrimp taste just as good and are often more economical. If clementines are in season, use these winsome and deliciously tangy-sweet, seedless fruit in the recipe. Otherwise, use seedless oranges for equally good results. Likewise, use the best olives you can find, making it as easy as possible on yourself by looking for an "olive bar" in your deli or produce section where many fine varieties are found already pitted. This Spanish-inspired main dish is wonderful with a simple rice pilaf studded with baby green peas and roasted red pepper. Caramel custard or flan is the ideal dessert.

- 3 large clementines or medium-sized seedless oranges
- ¼ cup olive oil
- 1¼ pounds jumbo or extra-large shrimp, peeled and deveined
- 4 large garlic cloves, finely chopped
- ⅛ to ¼ teaspoon crushed red pepper flakes, to taste
- ⅓ cup dry sherry
- 2 tablespoons sherry wine vinegar
- ¼ cup thinly sliced or chopped good quality black and/or green olives
- 3 tablespoons chopped flat-leaf parsley
  Salt and freshly ground pepper

From one of the clementines or oranges, squeeze ¼ cup of juice. Peel and section the remaining fruit.

In a large skillet, heat the oil and cook the shrimp, garlic, and red pepper flakes over medium heat until the shrimp just begin to turn pink, about 2 minutes. Add the orange segments and cook, stirring, for 1 minute. Add the sherry, vinegar, and juice, and simmer, stirring often, for 2 minutes. Stir in the olives and cook for 1 minute. Stir in the parsley. Season to taste with salt and lots of pepper, and serve.

herbed
clam
hash *4 servings*

Canned chopped (not minced) clams are fine for this recipe, but even better are fresh chopped clams from the fish market. This simple hash makes a warming supper for a cold winter's night, especially if you start with mugs of hot tomato soup, and serve the hash with steamed broccoli. If you want to be really traditional, top the hash with a fried or poached egg. The most comforting dessert on earth is probably chocolate pudding, especially with a big dollop of whipped cream.

6 bacon slices, diced
1 pound all-purpose russet potatoes, peeled and
   cut into ½-inch cubes
1 medium onion, chopped
1 medium red bell pepper, chopped
2 cups drained chopped fresh or canned clams
2 tablespoons chopped fresh marjoram
2 tablespoons chopped parsley
   Salt and freshly ground pepper

In a large skillet with a lid, cook the bacon over medium heat until crisp, about 4 minutes. Transfer to paper towels to drain. Add the potatoes to the drippings in the skillet and cook, stirring often, until softened and golden, about 5 minutes. Add the onion and bell pepper and cook until just softened, about 3 minutes. Stir in the clams and marjoram. Cover the skillet, reduce the heat to medium-low, and cook until the vegetables are softened, about 5 minutes. Uncover the skillet and stir in the parsley and cooked bacon. Raise the heat to medium-high and cook the hash, pressing down with the back of a spoon, until the bottom is crisp.

Season to taste with salt and pepper, then spoon it onto plates.

chesapeake crab cakes and mustard tartar sauce *4 servings*

In the Chesapeake Bay, where crab cooking is practically an art form, crab cakes are judged by how little filler is used in proportion to crabmeat. The quality of the crab itself also matters greatly, and so does the seafood seasoning, Old Bay being the one of choice. Although canned crabmeat is OK, this is the time to go for the good stuff—pasteurized fresh crab, found in the seafood department. Be sure to pick it over for any little bits of shell, and drain the crab well before combining with the other ingredients. The crab cakes will be loose and delicate, so when you cook them, turn only once and do it carefully. Serve the crab cakes and tartar sauce with shoestring French fries and a Bibb or Boston lettuce salad. This special supper needs an extraordinary dessert, so go all out and get a raspberry tart from the bakery.

- 1 large lemon
- ⅓ cup mayonnaise
- ½ cup finely chopped green onions
- 1¼ teaspoons dry mustard, preferably English-style hot mustard
- 1 large egg
- 1½ cups fresh bread crumbs from firm white or French bread
- 2 teaspoons Old Bay or other seafood seasoning
- ¾ pound fresh crabmeat, drained and picked over
- ¼ cup vegetable oil

Grate 1 teaspoon of zest and squeeze 2 tablespoons of juice from the lemon. Reserve.

In a small dish, stir together the mayonnaise, ¼ cup of the green onions, ½ teaspoon of the mustard, 1 tablespoon of the lemon juice, and ½ teaspoon of the zest. Refrigerate at least 10 minutes or until ready to serve.

In a medium mixing bowl, beat the egg, then stir in ¾ cup of the bread crumbs, the Old Bay seasoning, crabmeat, the remaining ¼ cup of green onions, ¾ teaspoon of mustard, 1 tablespoon of lemon juice and ½ teaspoon of zest. Place the remaining ¾ cup of bread crumbs on a plate. Divide the crab mixture into 8 portions, forming each into a loose cake about ¾ inch thick. Dip each cake into the bread crumbs to coat.

In a large skillet, heat the oil. Carefully place the crab cakes in the oil and cook over medium heat, undisturbed, until richly browned on the bottom, about 5 minutes. Carefully turn with a spatula and cook until the other side is richly browned, about 5 minutes more. (The crab cakes can be held in a 325-degree oven for up to 30 minutes before serving, if desired.)

Serve the crab cakes with the mustard tartar sauce.

mussels oreganata with leeks and cream

4 servings

Leeks are the gentle giants of the onion family, with a subtle flavor that is ideal for delicate seafood. Unlike the slim green onion, which is best crunchy and raw, leeks are at peak flavor with a brief, gentle cooking. Leeks tend to hold lots of sandy grit within their layers, especially toward the green parts. To clean them easily, trim to within an inch of the white part, then cut the leek in half lengthwise. Rinse the cut sides under cold water, separating the layers with your fingers until the water runs clear. Then dry the leeks well on paper towels before cooking them. Accompany this mussel and leek main course dish with an arugula salad tossed with a white wine vinaigrette, and be sure to serve lots of crusty French bread for sopping up the aromatic broth.

2 tablespoons butter
2 cups thinly sliced leeks (white and pale green parts only)
3 pounds mussels, scrubbed and debearded
1 cup dry white wine
1 cup heavy cream
½ cup bottled clam juice
3 tablespoons Pernod or other anise liqueur
3 tablespoons chopped fresh oregano
Salt and freshly ground pepper

In a large, deep skillet with a lid, heat the butter. Cook the leeks over medium-low heat, stirring often, until just softened, about 3 minutes. Add the mussels to the pan, then pour in the wine, cream, clam juice, Pernod, and half of the oregano. Cover the pan and bring the liquid to a boil over medium-high heat. Reduce the heat to medium-low and simmer until the mussels open, about 5 minutes.

Uncover and transfer the mussels to 4 shallow soup bowls, discarding any that have not opened. Stir the remaining half of the oregano into the broth, taste, and add salt and pepper. Bring the broth to a simmer, then pour it over the mussels, and serve.

fried oyster po' boy *4 servings*

Oyster Po' Boy is one of the most famous dishes in New Orleans, a city that knows its oysters. You can, of course, delete the sandwich part and just eat those crunchy coated, sweet and briny oysters all by themselves. In any case, there's no need to heat up a cauldron of hot oil to fry oysters. A frying pan and a mere ¼ inch of oil will produce the same results, and is a lot easier and quicker. This classic Emerald City street-food sandwich is a meal in itself. Finish off with the classic American "street-food" dessert, a double-decker ice cream cone—just make it pralines 'n' cream.

1 large lemon
⅓ cup mayonnaise
½ cup yellow cornmeal
1 teaspoon coarsely ground pepper
½ teaspoon salt
1 pint shucked oysters, drained (16 to 20 oysters)
 Vegetable oil for shallow frying
4 crusty hero or long sandwich rolls, split lengthwise
4 cups shredded romaine lettuce

Grate 1½ teaspoons of zest from the lemon and squeeze 1 tablespoon of juice. In a small dish, stir together the mayonnaise, lemon juice, and zest. Refrigerate at least 10 minutes or until ready to use.

On a plate, stir together the cornmeal, pepper, and salt. Dredge the oysters in the cornmeal mixture to coat completely. Arrange in a single layer on a plate.

In a large skillet, heat about ¼ inch of oil until a crust of bread sizzles when dropped in the oil. Fry the oysters, in two batches, and turning once, until browned and crusty, 2 to 3 minutes per side. Drain on paper towels.

Spread the cut sides of the rolls with the lemon mayonnaise, then arrange the oysters in the sandwich and top with shredded lettuce.

oysters
rockefeller
stew *4 servings*

All the classic ingredients are here—spinach, Worcestershire sauce, and oysters, of course. But this stew is considerably lighter than its incredibly rich namesake. Serve the stew with oyster crackers or French bread, or both. Then finish in true New Orleans style with pecan pie, saving the richness for the end!

3 tablespoons butter
1 medium onion, chopped
1 celery rib, thinly sliced (about 1 cup)
2 tablespoons all-purpose flour
4 cups milk
1 pint shucked oysters with their liquor
1 tablespoon Worcestershire sauce
2 cups baby spinach leaves (about 4 ounces)
1 tablespoon chopped fresh thyme
  Salt and freshly ground pepper

In a large, deep skillet, heat the butter. Cook the onion and celery over medium heat, stirring often, until softened, about 5 minutes. Stir in the flour and cook, stirring, for 1 minute. Slowly whisk in the milk and bring to a boil. Reduce the heat to medium-low, and add the oysters with their liquor and the Worcestershire sauce. Simmer until the oysters curl, 2 to 3 minutes. Add the spinach and thyme. Simmer until the spinach is barely wilted, about 1 minute. Season to taste with salt and pepper.

Serve the stew in shallow soup bowls.

pan-seared scallops with lemon-dill mignonette *4 servings*

Seared sea scallops are a restaurant specialty, largely because good sea scallops are now widely available and the dish makes such a spectacular presentation. The trick is to cook the scallops over high heat until golden on each side and just cooked through, and then make a quick, simple, yet sophisticated pan sauce. These scallops are especially pretty when served with roasted fingerling or small red potatoes, and pencil-thin asparagus spears. Since this is an elegant little dinner, go all out and have chocolate mousse for dessert.

  2 lemons
  3 tablespoons butter
  1 tablespoon vegetable oil
  1¼ pounds large sea scallops, patted dry
    Salt and freshly ground pepper
  ¼ cup chopped shallots
  ½ cup dry white wine
  1 tablespoon chopped fresh dill, plus sprigs for
    garnish

Grate 2 teaspoons of zest from 1½ of the lemons and squeeze 1 tablespoon of juice. Thinly slice the remaining ½ lemon. Reserve.

In a large skillet, heat 2 tablespoons of the butter and the oil. Season the scallops lightly with salt and pepper. Cook over medium-high heat until seared and golden on both sides and cooked through, turning the scallops once, 4 to 6 minutes total. Transfer the scallops to a plate.

Add the remaining 1 tablespoon of butter to the skillet and cook the shallots over medium heat for 30 seconds. Add the wine and reserved lemon juice and simmer for 1 minute. Stir in the chopped dill and reserved grated lemon zest and simmer for 30 seconds. Season to taste with salt and pepper.

Drizzle the scallops with the pan sauce, garnish with dill sprigs and lemon slices, and serve.

skillet-roasted clams with pancetta and peppers *4 servings*

If you can find tiny New Zealand clams, they will look especially pretty, but the more common littleneck, or any other medium-size hard-shell clams, or a combination of clams and mussels, will also be wonderful. Along the coast in Southern Italy, this meal would be enjoyed with a loaf of bread, some sliced ripe tomatoes dribbled with a little olive oil and balsamic vinegar, and a glass of red wine. Sounds like a good idea for American tables, too.

1 tablespoon olive oil
¼ pound pancetta or bacon, diced
1 medium onion, chopped
1 red bell pepper, chopped
2 large garlic cloves, finely chopped
3 pounds littleneck or New Zealand clams, scrubbed
1 cup dry red wine
¼ cup chopped fresh basil
  Salt and freshly ground pepper

In a large, deep skillet with a lid, heat the oil. Cook the pancetta over medium heat until crisp. Transfer to a plate and reserve. Add the onion and bell pepper to the drippings in the skillet. Cook, stirring often, until softened, about 5 minutes. Add the garlic and cook for 1 minute. Add the clams, then pour in the wine, and bring to a simmer. Cover the skillet, reduce the heat to medium-low, and simmer until the clams open, 5 to 10 minutes, depending on their size. Uncover and sprinkle with the basil.

Transfer the clams to 4 shallow soup plates, discarding any clams that have not opened. Season the broth with salt and pepper to taste, stir in the pancetta, then pour the broth over the clams.

meatless

Whether you're a vegetarian or just enjoy enhancing your weekly menu with an occasional meatless meal, this chapter will provide you with lots of quick and easy dishes—*quick and easy* being terms that have not always been synonymous with vegetarian cooking. In fact, in years past, making an acceptable (or even barely edible) meatless meal usually involved traipsing around, collecting an elaborate list of ingredients, and then spending long hours toiling away at the stove. But the food industry has been listening, and now supermarket shelves are filled with an ever-growing array of products that make cooking top-of-the-stove meatless meals a pleasure.

Since vegetarianism is a deeply rooted aspect of many cultures, this chapter is replete with our shortened renditions of some of the best meatless dishes from around the world. Seared Sesame Tofu with Crispy Vegetable Garnish (page 146), Ratatouille Provolone (page 149), and Pinto Bean Skillet Chili Sante Fe (page 153) are some stellar examples.

Canned beans, which are now available in such bountiful and delicious variety, are the featured ingredient in several recipes in this chapter, including an exotically seasoned Tunisian Eggplant and Chickpea Ragout (page 150), and Coconut Rice and Peas (page 156). Skillet Spinach Pesto Lasagne (page 148) is a breeze with no-boil lasagne noodles.

And then there are eggs—hardly new, of course, but newly respectable (having lost some of their naughty high-cholesterol reputation), and the absolutely perfect beginning to many a meatless skillet supper. We offer you four master egg recipes and tons of variations on those themes.

recipes

seared sesame tofu with crispy vegetable garnish *4 servings*

Tofu is graded and labeled according to its moisture content. *Silken* is the softest tofu and *extra firm* is the driest. The latter has an almost meaty texture and is an excellent choice for most sautéing. As for the vegetable garnish, you could easily use just about any combination of crisp vegetables, such as julienned carrots, slivered red onions, and shredded cucumber. All you really need to round out this elegant entrée is something like a brown rice or couscous salad. A pretty fruit dessert such as scoops of coconut ice cream topped with berries would be a nice way to end the meal.

1 pound extra-firm tofu, cut into ½-inch-thick slices
Salt and freshly ground pepper
½ cup sesame seeds
1 cup slivered green onions
1 cup slivered red or yellow bell peppers, or a combination of the two
1¼ cups bean sprouts
6 tablespoons peanut oil or roasted garlic-flavored vegetable oil
2 tablespoons finely chopped fresh ginger
⅓ cup rice wine vinegar

Dry the tofu thoroughly on paper towels and sprinkle it on all sides with salt and pepper. Spread out the sesame seeds on a plate and dredge the tofu slices in the seeds to coat all sides. In a bowl, toss together the green onions, bell peppers, and bean sprouts to combine.

In a large skillet, heat 3 tablespoons of the oil over medium-high heat. Add the tofu, reduce the heat to medium, and cook, turning once, until the tofu is a rich golden brown on both sides, about 6 minutes total. Transfer to a plate, leaving any sesame seeds that have fallen off in the pan. (They will become part of the sauce.)

Add the remaining 3 tablespoons of oil to the pan. Add the ginger and cook over medium-high heat, stirring, for 1 minute. Add the vinegar, bring to a boil, and remove from the heat. Season to taste with salt and pepper.

Mound the vegetables on dinner plates, lean the tofu against the vegetables, and drizzle with the pan sauce.

skillet spinach pesto lasagne *4 servings*

This skillet cooking method turns lasagne making into an absolute breeze! While the method might seem unorthodox, it works just beautifully—the only requirement being a skillet that is at least eleven inches in diameter and two inches deep so as to comfortably contain the sauce. Using readily available "no-boil" lasagne noodles (or, even better, fresh pasta sheets) eliminates entirely one of the messiest steps of making lasagne. Just add garlic bread and a mixed mesclun salad dressed with balsamic vinaigrette, and you've got a simply splendid meal that everyone will love. Peppermint stick ice cream drizzled with hot fudge sauce might be an appropriate finish.

- 1¼ cups ricotta cheese
- ½ cup grated Pecorino Romano or Parmesan cheese
- ½ cup purchased pesto sauce
- 1½ cups shredded mozzarella cheese
- ½ teaspoon salt
- ½ teaspoon pepper
- One 26-ounce jar chunky tomato sauce (3 cups)
- 6 no-boil lasagne noodles, or 6 strips fresh lasagne
- 3 cups baby spinach leaves (about 6 ounces)

In a large bowl, whisk together the ricotta, Pecorino Romano, pesto, half the mozzarella, and the salt and pepper.

In the bottom of a large, deep skillet with a lid, spread one third of the tomato sauce in an even layer. Arrange 3 of the noodles over the sauce, breaking or cutting them up if necessary to make one layer. Drop half the cheese mixture, by spoonfuls, over the noodles and spread with a rubber spatula to make a fairly even layer. Spread half the spinach leaves over the cheese.

Repeat the layers with another third of the sauce, the remaining 3 noodles, the remaining ricotta mixture, and the remaining spinach. Top with the last third of the sauce, and sprinkle with the remaining half of the mozzarella.

Place the skillet on the stove and bring to a boil over high heat. Cover, reduce the heat to medium-low, and cook, regulating the heat if necessary so that the sauce is bubbling gently around the edges the whole time, until the noodles are tender and the cheese on top is melted, about 25 minutes. (The lasagne can be cooked up to 1 hour ahead and kept at cool room temperature. Reheat for a few minutes over low heat.)

Let the lasagne stand for 5 minutes before cutting into wedges to serve.

ratatouille provolone *4 servings*

We invariably think of making ratatouille when the garden or farmers' market is bursting with all those glorious, height-of-summer eggplants, squashes, and peppers. Here, by simply topping that ratatouille with a layer of deliciously pungent provolone, it becomes an instant main course. As in all the simplest recipes, the quality of the ingredients makes a real difference, so be sure to shop for the best imported provolone available. Add a salad of greens sprinkled with meaty black olives, a loaf of crusty peasant bread, and you've got a terrific summertime, or anytime, supper.

      ¼ cup olive oil, preferably extra-virgin
      1 medium-large eggplant (about 1 pound), cut into
            1-inch cubes
      1 large green bell pepper, coarsely chopped
      1 large yellow squash, thinly sliced
         Salt and freshly ground pepper
      2 garlic cloves, finely chopped
   One 14½-ounce can Italian-style diced tomatoes
      ⅓ cup slivered or torn fresh basil
      6 ounces sliced or shredded provolone cheese

In a large skillet with a lid, heat the oil over medium-high heat. Add the eggplant, bell pepper, and squash, season generously with salt and pepper, and stir well to combine. Cover the pan, reduce the heat to medium, and cook, stirring every few minutes, until the eggplant begins to soften and brown, 10 to 15 minutes.

Add the garlic and cook, stirring, for 1 minute. Add the tomatoes and bring to a boil, stirring. Reduce the heat to medium and simmer, uncovered, until most of the liquid is absorbed and evaporated, about 10 minutes. Stir in the basil and season to taste with salt and pepper. (The ratatouille can be made up to several hours ahead to this point and refrigerated. Reheat gently.)

Spread the cheese over the ratatouille in an even layer. Cover the pan and cook over medium-low to medium heat until the cheese melts and the ratatouille is bubbly around the edges, 3 to 5 minutes.

Cut into wedges or spoon out of the skillet onto individual plates.

tunisian eggplant and chickpea ragout *4 servings*

Sweet spices (in the form of pumpkin pie spice mixture) combine with cumin and cayenne to scent this mixed vegetable mélange. Steamed couscous is the natural accompaniment, with perhaps a cucumber and yogurt salad on the side. A platter of Middle Eastern honey pastries is just the right dessert.

¼ cup plus 1 tablespoon fruity olive oil
1 medium-large eggplant (about 1 pound), peeled
   and cut into rough ¾-inch cubes
1 large onion, chopped
1 green bell pepper, chopped
   Salt and freshly ground pepper
3 garlic cloves, finely chopped
2 teaspoons ground cumin
2 teaspoons pumpkin pie spice
½ teaspoon cayenne pepper
One 28-ounce can diced tomatoes
½ cup dry white wine
2 cups drained chickpeas
½ cup chopped parsley

In a large, deep skillet, heat the oil. Add the eggplant, onion, and bell pepper, and sprinkle with salt and pepper. Cook over medium to medium-high heat, stirring often, until the eggplant begins to soften and brown, about 10 minutes. Add the garlic and cook, stirring, for 1 minute. Add the cumin, pumpkin pie spice, and cayenne, and cook, stirring, for 1 minute.

Add the tomatoes and wine, and bring to a boil. Reduce the heat to medium and simmer, uncovered, for 5 minutes. Add the chickpeas and half the parsley and continue to simmer until the eggplant is very tender and the juices are reduced and thickened to a stewlike consistency, about 10 minutes. (The ragout can be made several hours ahead, covered, and refrigerated. Reheat gently.)

Season to taste with salt and pepper, sprinkle with the remaining half of the parsley, and serve.

portobellos with sherry-scallion gravy *4 servings*

These delicious giant mushrooms are so dense and meaty that they're akin to steak. They are wonderful served with buttered and herbed egg noodles (all the better to sop up the lovely gravy) along with a sliced tomato salad dressed with balsamic vinaigrette.

4 large portobello mushrooms (5 to 6 ounces each), stems trimmed to ½ inch
¼ cup plus 2 tablespoons olive oil
Salt and freshly ground pepper
1 large lemon, halved
2 tablespoons butter
¼ cup thinly sliced scallions
1½ tablespoons all-purpose flour
¾ cup dry sherry
½ cup grated manchego or Asiago cheese

Place the mushrooms on a plate, drizzle or brush with ¼ cup of the oil, and season on both sides with salt and pepper.

Squeeze 1 tablespoon of juice from one of the lemon halves. Cut the remaining half into 4 wedges.

In a large skillet with a lid, heat the remaining 2 tablespoons of oil. Place the mushrooms in the pan, cap side down, and cook over medium heat for 5 minutes. Turn the mushrooms, reduce the heat to medium-low, and cover the pan. Cook the mushrooms until tender, 10 to 15 minutes. Transfer to a plate. If the pan drippings are burned, wipe the pan out with a paper towel.

Add the butter to the skillet, raise the heat to medium-high, and add about two thirds of the scallions. Cook, stirring, for 2 minutes. Sprinkle with the flour and cook, stirring, for 1 minute. Gradually whisk in the sherry and ¼ cup of water. Bring to a boil, whisking constantly, and cook until the gravy is smooth and bubbly. Add the reserved lemon juice and season to taste with salt and pepper.

Ladle some of the gravy on each of 4 plates and place a mushroom in the center. Sprinkle with the cheese and the remaining chopped scallions. Garnish with a lemon wedge and serve.

pinto bean
skillet chili
sante fe *4 servings*

This chili is one of our meatless mainstays for our children's, and our own, vegetarian friends. We think it's
best made with pinto beans, which have a creamy texture and slightly sweet, earthy flavor, but kidney beans
will work well, too. Steamed yellow or white rice, a
basket of warm tortillas, and a salad of romaine and red
onion sprinkled with toasted sunflower seeds are excellent accompaniments. A creamy flan topped with
seasonal fruit would be the perfect dessert.

¼ cup light olive oil
1 large onion, coarsely chopped
1 large green bell pepper, coarsely chopped
2½ tablespoons good quality chili powder
1 cup vegetable or chicken broth
Two 14½-ounce cans Mexican- or chili-style diced
       tomatoes
3 cups drained pinto beans
   Salt and freshly ground pepper
2 cups shredded pepper Jack cheese (8 ounces)

In a large, deep skillet, heat the oil. Add the onion
and bell pepper and cook over medium-high heat,
stirring frequently, until the vegetables begin to
soften, about 5 minutes. Sprinkle with the chili
powder and cook, stirring, for 1 minute. Add the
broth, tomatoes, and beans, and bring to a boil. Using
the back of a large spoon, mash about one quarter of
the beans against the side of the pan. (This helps
thicken the chili.) Reduce the heat to medium and
simmer, uncovered, for 10 minutes until the liquid is
slightly reduced and thickened. (The chili can be
made up to 2 days ahead to this point and refrigerated. Reheat gently.)

   Season to taste with salt and pepper. Ladle into
shallow soup bowls, sprinkle with cheese, and serve.

meatless
mexican
monte cristos *4 servings*

The classic Monte Cristo sandwich includes chicken or another meat among the layers. We say cheese only, please, especially when it's flavorful pepper Jack, studded with zingy jalapeño peppers. This is the perfect comfy supper, especially when preceded by a mug of pea soup and then accompanied by crinkle-cut potato chips and crisp carrot and celery sticks.

- 6 large eggs
- ½ teaspoon salt
- ¼ teaspoon pepper
- ¼ cup chopped cilantro
- ¾ pound pepper Jack cheese, sliced or shredded
- 8 slices firm, chewy bread
- 4 tablespoons butter
- 1 cup good quality chunky salsa

In a shallow dish, lightly beat the eggs with ¼ cup of water and the salt and pepper. Stir in the cilantro.

Make 4 sandwiches by layering the cheese between the slices of bread.

In a large skillet, heat the butter. Dip the sandwiches in the egg mixture, turning to coat both sides of the bread. Cook over medium heat, in two batches if necessary, turning once, until both sides are crusty and golden brown and the cheese is melted, 5 to 8 minutes total.

Cut each sandwich in half and serve, topped with the salsa.

coconut
rice
and peas *4 servings*

We know them as kidney beans, but in this scrumptious dish they're called peas, as in rice 'n' peas, or peas 'n' rice, depending on which Caribbean island is claiming it. Coconut milk adds flavor and richness, jalapeños contribute heat, and the whole dish melds together beautifully, transporting you to a sun-drenched, calypso-playing West Indian isle. Just add an avocado and tomato salad, a basket of hot corn-bread, and for dessert, some cooling tropical fruit sorbet and a plate of crisp ginger cookies.

 2 tablespoons butter
1¼ cups thinly sliced green onions
 1 cup long-grain white rice
 2 cups vegetable broth or chicken broth, plus additional if necessary
 1 cup canned unsweetened coconut milk
 2 cups drained kidney beans
 ¼ teaspoon ground allspice
 1 teaspoon salt
 ½ teaspoon pepper
 2 tablespoons chopped fresh thyme, plus sprigs for garnish
 1 tablespoon minced jalapeño peppers

In a large, deep skillet with a lid, heat the butter. Add half the green onions and cook over medium-high heat, stirring, for 1 minute. Add the rice and cook, stirring, until the grains begin to turn opaque, about 3 minutes. Add the broth, coconut milk, beans, all-spice, salt, and pepper. Bring to a boil, stirring to blend in the coconut milk. Reduce the heat to low and cook, covered, for 10 minutes.

Stir in the thyme and jalapeños and finish cooking the dish over medium heat, uncovered, until the rice is tender and most of the liquid is absorbed, about 10 minutes. If the rice is not quite cooked and the mixture looks dry, add more broth or water, ¼ cup at a time. (The dish can be cooked up to several hours ahead and held at cool room temperature or refrigerated. Reheat in a microwave.)

With a fork, stir in the remaining half of the green onions. Season to taste with salt and pepper and garnish with thyme sprigs before serving.

scrambled eggs and variations
4 servings

Our informal neighborhood poll revealed that scrambled is the most favored egg dish. It probably has to do with its homey, comforting familiarity. Those fluffy, tender mounds of golden egg just waiting to be scooped up with a wedge of crusty toast, forked with a slice of crisp salty bacon, or even slathered with ketchup (yes, we have one kid who holds to the ketchup tradition and it's not bad) evoke cozy childhood memories. And they're not just for breakfast, either. Scrambled eggs, frizzled ham, and stewed tomatoes are a cold-weather late night supper that takes about ten minutes and does more for the soul than an hour on the psychiatrist's couch. Finish the meal with warm gingerbread with lemon curd spooned over each slice, and the psychiatrist will have to go out of business.

The secret to moist, tender scrambled eggs is slow cooking and slow stirring with a wooden spoon. Since the eggs cool fast, and cold scrambled eggs are just plain awful, a really nice touch for serving is to warm the plates, either in a low oven or plate warmer, or by rinsing them under hot water. If there are only two of you for supper, simply halve the ingredients and use an eight- or nine-inch skillet.

  8 large eggs
  3 tablespoons milk or half-and-half
  ½ teaspoon salt
  ¼ to ½ teaspoon freshly ground pepper, to taste
  2 tablespoons butter

In a mixing bowl, use a fork or whisk to blend together the eggs, milk, salt, and pepper until the ingredients are well blended, but not foamy.

In a large skillet, melt the butter over medium heat until it begins to sizzle. Reduce the heat to medium-low and pour in the eggs. Cook, stirring slowly and constantly with a wooden spoon or spatula, until the eggs form soft, fluffy curds, 5 to 8 minutes. If the eggs begin to stick or brown in the pan, reduce the heat to low.

If you are making a variation, stir in the additional ingredients, taste, and adjust the seasoning. Serve immediately, preferably on warm plates.

variations:

Add 1 or 2 tablespoons of chopped fresh herbs, such as tarragon, thyme, parsley, dill, chervil, basil, chives, or cilantro.

Add up to ½ cup shredded sharp cheddar, Swiss, Monterey Jack, or other full-flavored cheese. Or add up to ¼ cup grated Parmesan or Romano cheese.

Add 2 ounces of cubed plain or flavored cream cheese, which will not only enrich the eggs, but also keep them creamy for up to 15 minutes in a chafing or warming dish.

Add up to 1 cup mixed cooked vegetables, such as sliced green onions, asparagus tips, broccoli florets, diced bell peppers, or sliced mushrooms.

basic
omelet and
variations *1 serving, which can be doubled ad infinitum*

An omelet serves one. Fortunately, each takes only about one minute to make, so it's easy to serve two or even four people, especially if you have two pans going at once. Since our families really like omelets and we like skillets, we use our omelet pan, a 7-inch nonstick pan with sloping sides, and our 8-inch skillet, which is not nonstick, and looks a lot like an omelet pan, but without the fancy name. We add butter to both of the pans either way. The nonstick coating doesn't eliminate the need for fat, but it does make it a lot easier to get the omelet out of the pan. So if you are going to buy an omelet pan, go for a high-quality nonstick one. Depending upon your filling, the accompaniments to an omelet supper can be a big tossed salad and rolls or a cornbread of some sort. Since omelets are soft and warming, we like a cool, crunchy dessert, such as lemon sorbet and crisp sugar cookies.

2 or 3 large eggs

$\frac{1}{4}$ teaspoon salt

$\frac{1}{4}$ teaspoon coarsely ground pepper

2 teaspoons butter or olive oil

$\frac{1}{4}$ cup filling of choice (see page 160), warmed or at room temperature

In a small bowl, use a fork to blend together the eggs, 1 tablespoon of water, the salt, and pepper until just blended, but not foamy or runny.

Melt the butter or oil in a 7- to 9-inch skillet or omelet pan over medium heat until sizzling. Reduce the heat to medium-low, then swirl the butter or oil to coat the bottom of the pan, and pour the eggs into the center. Cook, undisturbed, for 10 to 15 seconds, until the bottom is set, then use a spatula to carefully lift up the edges and tilt the pan to let the uncooked top run beneath the set eggs. Do this once more, until the top of the omelet is nearly set, with just a little runny part left. The entire procedure will take only 1 to 1$\frac{1}{2}$ minutes.

Spoon the filling down the center of the omelet, then use the spatula to fold one third of the omelet over the filling. Next, if you are adept, flip over the omelet, folding the remaining third over the filling, and sliding the omelet out of the pan onto a plate. If you are not an omelet gymnast, use the spatula to fold the remaining third over the filling, then slide the omelet onto a plate, attempting to turn the folded side underneath as you slide. This might take a little practice, so make a couple of omelets for yourself before you attempt theatrics for company.

continued on page 160

omelet fillings:

Crumbled cooked bacon, cheddar cheese, and chopped
sweet onion

Chopped, cooked broccoli rabe, garlic, and grated
Parmesan cheese

Chopped, cooked spinach, nutmeg, and grated
Swiss cheese

Cooked corn, chopped red and green bell pepper, and
grated Monterey Jack cheese

Cooked black beans, ground cumin, and chopped
red onion

Chopped smoked salmon and dill, mixed with
sour cream

Crumbled feta cheese, chopped mint, and slivered
romaine lettuce

Chopped or sliced olives, chopped basil, and chopped
roasted red pepper

Thinly sliced pepperoni, grated mozzarella cheese, and
diced fresh tomato

Chutney, curry powder, and cooked rice

Diced fried potatoes and onion, chopped fresh thyme,
and bottled chili sauce or ketchup

Slivered ham, cooked collard greens, and hot-pepper
sauce

Crumbled cooked Italian sausage, chopped roasted
peppers, and chopped fresh marjoram

Diced tomato, cubed mozzarella, and slivered basil

Cooked asparagus tips and baby green peas, and
chopped lemon zest

Diced zucchini, chopped mint, and crumbled
goat cheese

fried eggs
and variations *2 servings*

We love fried eggs for supper, especially fried egg sandwiches made with whole-wheat toast, just a little chili sauce, and a sprinkling of sharp cheddar cheese. The yolk should be a little runny so it soaks into the toast, and the white should be tinged with a bit of gold for extra flavor. If you are concerned about eating undercooked eggs, you can buy pasteurized eggs. They are worth the trouble for fried eggs since hard yolks ruin the dish.

Getting the tinge of gold in the whites is the tricky part. Eggs need to be cooked slowly over gentle heat, or they toughen, but the golden tinge needs a higher heat, so we turn it up to medium for only a few seconds toward the end of the cooking time when the egg white is already set. Over-easy eggs require more skill, and even with a wide spatula and a quick flip, the yolk might just break. If you are finicky, just start again—eggs are cheap and the cooking is quick. But we don't do that. We just eat those broken-yolk eggs. They taste fine and the sandwich hides the fracture, anyway.

Fried eggs have a kinship with hash-brown potatoes, and that's how we like to serve them. A generous green salad is nice for supper, and the end to such a home-style meal ought to be oatmeal cookies, don't you think? The recipe serves two, and if you need more, just make it again.

    1 tablespoon butter
    4 large eggs
    ¼ teaspoon salt, or more to taste
    ¼ teaspoon pepper, or more to taste

In a large skillet, melt the butter over medium heat until it begins to sizzle, then reduce the heat to medium-low. Meanwhile, break the eggs, one at a time, into a small cup. As each egg is broken, slowly slide it into the sizzling butter. (Doing this slowly will help keep the yolk intact and centered in the pool of white.) Sprinkle evenly with the salt and pepper.

Cook the eggs over medium-low heat until the whites are nearly set, about 4 minutes. Raise the heat to medium and continue to cook until the whites are just set and the edges are tinged with gold, about 1 minute more. These are sunny-side-up eggs. If you want them over easy, use a large spatula to flip the entire egg over and cook until the top of the yolk turns one shade lighter and just begins to set, about 15 seconds.

Serve the eggs immediately.

variations:

Serve the eggs sandwiched between slices of whole-wheat toast with a little chili sauce and a sprinkling of cheddar cheese.

Serve the eggs atop crisp corn tortillas (tostada shells) with shredded Monterey Jack cheese and warmed salsa.

Sprinkle the eggs with up to 1 tablespoon of chopped fresh herbs such as chervil, parsley, chives, tarragon, dill, or thyme, at the same time that you season with the salt and pepper.

Serve the eggs atop corned beef hash, or hash-brown potatoes, or potato pancakes.

basic frittata
and variations *4 servings*

A frittata is a sort of thick omelet that cooks slowly in the pan until it is set and can be cut in wedges. Because of the slow cooking and the many flavorful ingredients added to frittatas, they are also good at room temperature, though we aren't crazy about them left overnight and warmed up. Still, they are easy to make and can be held at cool room temperature or briefly refrigerated for up to 4 hours, which makes them a terrific make-ahead egg dish for parties. The Spanish always serve their classic tortilla, which is really a potato frittata, at room temperature as part of a tapas buffet. Cut into small pieces, frittatas make great predinner nibbles, but we mostly like to serve them as the main course since they are so simple, enormously versatile, and well liked by everyone.

Classic French frittatas are flipped in the skillet to brown the top. That's really tricky, so if you want a browned top, we recommend that you run the skillet under the broiler for a few seconds. In this recipe, how-ever, you don't need the broiler since the top is finished with a melting of cheese.

- 2 tablespoons butter or olive oil
- 1½ cups filling of choice (see facing page)
- 8 large eggs
- ½ teaspoon salt, or more or less, depending upon the filling
- ½ teaspoon coarsely ground pepper, or more or less, depending upon the filling
- 1 cup shredded or grated cheese (see facing page)

In a large skillet with a lid, melt the butter over medium heat. If the filling needs cooking (such as onions), cook in the butter or oil over medium heat, then spread evenly over the bottom of the pan. If the filling does not need cooking, spread it over the bottom of the pan and warm for 1 or 2 minutes.

Use a fork or whisk to blend the eggs, salt, and pepper. Pour the eggs evenly over the filling, tilting the pan to cover the filling completely. Cook, undis-turbed, until the bottom and edges begin to look set, about 3 minutes. Use a spatula to carefully lift up the edges, allowing uncooked egg to run underneath. Repeat the lifting once, then cover the pan, and reduce the heat to medium-low or low depending upon your stove. Cook, undisturbed, until the top is nearly set, 11 to 13 minutes.

Uncover and sprinkle evenly with the cheese. Cover the pan again, and cook until the top is set and the cheese is melted, 2 to 3 minutes.

Let the frittata stand in the skillet for about 30 seconds, then use a spatula to loosen the edges from the pan. Cut into 8 wedges and serve warm or at room temperature, 2 wedges per person.

frittata
fillings
and cheese
toppings:

Cooked sliced asparagus, diced ham; grated Swiss
  cheese on top

Corn, chopped red and green bell pepper; grated
  pepper Jack cheese on top

Crumbled cooked sausage, chopped roasted red
  peppers, chopped fresh rosemary; grated fontina
  cheese on top

Chopped smoked salmon, chopped fresh dill,
  chopped red onion; grated Gouda cheese on top

Coarsely chopped cooked broccoli rabe, chopped
  garlic, slivered sun-dried tomato; grated provolone
  cheese on top

Chopped cooked collard greens, crumbled cooked
  bacon, dry or Dijon mustard; grated cheddar cheese
  on top

Diced fried potatoes, cooked chopped onion;
  chopped fresh rosemary, grated smoked mozzarella
  cheese on top

Cooked broccoli florets and sliced stems, chopped
  red bell pepper, chopped roasted garlic; crumbled
  goat cheese on top

index

table of equivalents

The exact equivalents in the following tables have been rounded for convenience.

liquid / dry measures

U.S.	metric
¼ teaspoon	1.25 milliliters
½ teaspoon	2.5 milliliters
1 teaspoon	5 milliliters
1 tablespoon (3 teaspoons)	15 milliliters
1 fluid ounce (2 tablespoons)	30 milliliters
¼ cup	60 milliliters
⅓ cup	80 milliliters
½ cup	120 milliliters
1 cup	240 milliliters
1 pint (2 cups)	480 milliliters
1 quart (4 cups, 32 ounces)	960 milliliters
1 gallon (4 quarts)	3.84 liters
1 ounce (by weight)	28 grams
1 pound	454 grams
2.2 pounds	1 kilogram

length

U.S.	metric
⅛ inch	3 millimeters
¼ inch	6 millimeters
½ inch	12 millimeters
1 inch	2.5 centimeters

oven temperature

fahrenheit	celsius	gas
250	120	½
275	140	1
300	150	2
325	160	3
350	180	4
375	190	5
400	200	6
425	220	7
450	230	8
475	240	9
500	260	10